GENERALSHIP

HR Leadership
in a Time of War

and more ...

"Human Resources is now facing extraordinary challenges. This demanding time requires the kind of bold, thoughtful and thorough leadership suggested by 'Generalship.' HR leaders will benefit enormously by using this book and its concepts as their model for leading a function fighting to change and prevail in the face of these challenges."

> —Guy Patton
> Executive Vice President-Human Resources
> Fidelity Investments

"Don't miss this book. It will change both how you see yourself and your role in the world of work. It's Machiavelli's *The Prince* and Covey's *The 7 Habits of Highly Effective People* . . . all rolled into one for the HR profession."

> —Donna Introcaso
> former VP/HR
> iVillage and Winstar Communications

"Now, I know why HR professionals are called 'generalists' and CEOs are referred to as 'captains of industry.' This book is a must read on HR leadership, not only for HR practitioners, but for every CEO and Company Director, as well."

> —Robert S. Nadel
> President
> Nadel Consulting/HR Spectrum

"I loved the premise and absolutely agree with the notion of HR being in a 'War for Relevancy.' I have been in HR nearly 25 years and . . . felt energized after reading your book . . . your words made me rethink my attitude and renew the fight."

> —Jeannie Mongiello
> Vice President-Staffing
> Prudential Financial

Also by Peter Weddle

Career Fitness
How to Find, Win & Keep the Job You Want in the 1990's

CliffsNotes: Finding a Job on the Web

CliffsNotes: Writing a Great Resume

Computer-Based Instruction in Military Environments
(with Robert J. Seidel)

Electronic Resumes for the New Job Market

Internet Resumes: Take the Net to Your Next Job

Postcards From Space
Being the Best in Online Recruitment & HR Management
(2001, 2003)

T'is of Thee
A Son's Search for the Meaning of Patriotism

WEDDLE's InfoNotes (WIN): Writing a Great Resume

WEDDLE's Recruiter's Guide to Employment Web Sites
(annually, 1999-2004)

WEDDLE's Job Seeker's Guide to Employment Web Sites
(annually, 2000-2004)

WEDDLE's Directory of Employment-Related Internet Sites
(annually, 2002-2004)

WEDDLE's Recruiter's Guide to Association Web Sites

GENERALSHIP

HR Leadership
In a Time of War

Peter Weddle

WEDDLE's
www.weddles.com
2052 Shippan Avenue
Stamford, CT 06902
Where People Matter Most

*"We must be the change
we wish to see in the world."*

—Gandhi

CONTENTS

Battlefield Tales of Great War Time Leaders
and the Lessons They Hold for HR Professionals

for
Human Resource professionals
everywhere

the hope
for great leadership
in America's enterprises

GENERALSHIP

HR Leadership
in a Time of War

ACKNOWLEDGEMENTS

Many of the concepts presented in this book were developed through my personal interactions with current and former General Officers in the U.S. Army. During the years 1982-1988, I had the privilege of serving two terms as a member of the U.S. Army Science Board, an appointed position with the protocol rank of General Officer. In that position, I worked with some of this nation's finest generals and military leaders, including General George S. Blanchard, former Commander-in-Chief, U.S. Army Europe; General Maxwell R. Thurman, former Commander-in-Chief, U.S. Southern Command; and Brigadier General Paul D. Phillips, former Deputy Assistant Secretary of the Army for Manpower.

In addition, as a West Point graduate, I went to school and lived with, learned from and served among many of the General Officers leading today's U.S. Army. These fine officers include my roommate, Major General Dell L. Dailey, my company-mate, Major General Robert E. Armbruster, and my classmates, Lieutenant General Narcisco L. Abaya, Major General Joseph L. Bergantz, Brigadier General John S. Brown, Brigadier General James. J. Grazioplene, Major General Franklin L. Hagenbeck, Lieutenant General William J. Lennox, Jr., Major General Michael D. Maples, Lieutenant General Thomas F.

Metz, Lieutenant General Boonsrang Niumpradit, Brigadier General Christopher C. Shoemaker, Brigadier General Andrew W. Smoak, Major General Charles H. Swannack, Jr., and Major General Hans A. Van Winkle. I greatly admire what they do for our country and am profoundly grateful for the quality of their leadership in a time of war.

This book has also been shaped by research. I am indebted to a number of military and civilian scholars who have explored the concept of generalship and the attributes of generals in a time of war. These individuals include General Montgomery C. Meigs, Colonel R. Ernest Dupuy, Major John M. Vermillion, Ross Davies, Mike Iavarone, Charles M. Province, David Sargent, and Thomas Smith, as well as researchers at the Rand Corporation and Spartacus Educational. I learned much from the quality of their scholarship and their insights.

Finally, it is important to note that any misstatement of fact or misinterpretation of information that appears in this book is mine alone, and I take full responsibility for all such errors. I do that, of course, because it is the right thing to do, but also because, as you will read, it is one of the seven attributes of generalship in a time of war.

A BRIEF PRIMER
ON THE RANK OF GENERAL

The commissioned officer corps of the United States Army is organized into ten ranks. The vast majority of officers, however, spend their entire careers working in one of six ranks. In order of increasing seniority, they are:

- Second Lieutenant
- First Lieutenant
- Captain
- Major
- Lieutenant Colonel
- Colonel

A very small number of elite officers are promoted to the rank of General Officer. These officers are the senior leaders of the Army. They are its executives. They direct all other officers in the Army, who, in turn, lead the soldiers in their units.

Among General Officers, there are four ranks. They are listed in the table below, in order of increasing seniority.

Rank	Insignia
Brigadier General	★
Major General	★★

| Lieutenant General | ★★★ |
| General | ★★★★ |

During World War II, a special rank of General of the Army was created. Only five people have ever been appointed to this rank; they are Generals of the Army George C. Marshall, Douglas A. MacArthur, Dwight D. Eisenhower, Henry H. Arnold and Omar N. Bradley. The insignia of General of the Army is five stars in a circular pattern.

Although not always true, Brigadier Generals typically command independent brigades and serve as the deputy commanders of divisions. Major Generals command divisions, a fighting unit of approximately 10-15,000 soldiers. Lieutenant Generals command corps, a combat unit composed of several divisions. And, Generals command armies that include two or more corps as well as naval and air force units.

A Final Note: Although every General deserves to be recognized by his or her specific rank (e.g., Brigadier General, Major General), doing so would be cumbersome in recounting the vignettes included in this book. Therefore, I have used the title of "General" for all of the General Officers who are mentioned.

INTRODUCTION

Today, Human Resource Management (HR) is a noble profession searching for answers. Why isn't what we do more valued by the enterprise? Why are our programs and staff the last to be funded and the first to be cut? Why doesn't HR have a chair at the table where decisions get made? And why, as a consequence, are we and our work marginalized, trivialized and disrespected by so many leaders in so many organizations?

Yes, yes, I know; such issues are not your experience. That's fine . . . if it's true. Unfortunately, however, many of us in the HR profession suffer from the NIMO condition, the Not In My Organization response to any critical statement made about the status of the HR profession and/or its role in the modern American enterprise. Regardless of their accuracy or justification, we leap to the barricades to defend ourselves and our employers against these scurrilous attacks. And for what? Have our efforts in any way enhanced our stature, improved our standing or upgraded our security in the vast majority of companies? In my view, they have not.

Moreover, even if an employer has a fulsome respect for HR, the NIMO response is problematic. Why? Because Chief Executive Officers come and go at warp speed these days, and when they do, the role that HR plays in any specific organization can change overnight. In addition, we in the HR profession are also on the move—voluntarily and otherwise—and when we join a new organization, we often quickly discover that our condition has radically changed. All of a sudden, it is more accurately and ominously described as DIMO . . . Definitely In My Organization.

The questions raised above, therefore, are important to every HR leader and professional, regardless of their personal situation at the moment. They represent a grave threat to each and all of us. For HR professionals—most of whom are refreshingly optimistic—that reality may be hard to accept. Indeed, barely a month goes by without some author, in an HR publication somewhere, opining that "things are getting better." And, I suppose, they are. But the pace of that improvement is so glacial that it will be the Twenty-Second Century before we see any substantive progress in HR's position in the enterprise.

All of which is to say that—as difficult and even unpleasant as it may be—we must address those questions, and we must do so now. This book, however, doesn't presume to have all of the answers. What it does offer is an uncommon perspective on what's causing the questions to be raised in the first place, on the root source of our perpetually diminutive position. And, from that perspective, it develops an unconventional prescription for how we can change our standing.

You see, I don't believe that HR's position in the enterprise will ever improve because the CEO suddenly sees the light or because the business case finally becomes clear and compelling to the Chief Financial Officer. No, it will only happen when we stop seeing ourselves as the victims of circumstances beyond our control and, instead, re-imagine ourselves as the agents of the change we seek to achieve. Said another way, we will never change the views of those outside our profession until we, inside the profession, change our own views about who we are and what we do.

Why is that change necessary? Because the world around us has changed. We must adopt or become endangered, or more accurately, irrelevant. As Charles Darwin wrote, "It's not the strongest of the species, nor the most intelligent, that survive; it's the one most responsive to change." So, that is my uncommon perspective. The only way to change the world view of our profession is to change our profession's view of its role in the world.

But what is that new view? What adjustments must we make? These are the root issues that we must address. They are our start point, and they lead directly to my unconventional prescription.

I am a West Point graduate, a former officer in a U.S. Army combat unit, so I can best describe my notion with a military metaphor. Now, some have told me that such an approach is a bad idea, because . . . well, the HR profession is a field largely populated by women, and women don't go to war. My response to that view is two-fold: first, women are soldiers today, and they are engaged in combat all over the world on behalf of our nation. And second, women in the workforce may not be soldiers, but they are definitely fighting . . . to break through the glass ceiling in corporate America, to establish their right to be whatever they can be in the world of work.

So, the military metaphor may be a little unusual, but it is clearly applicable to the HR profession. And traditionally, we in the profession—both leaders and led—have worked hard to be "good soldiers." Day in-day out, we salute and follow the directions we are given. "Do more with less," our leaders say. And we reply, "Yes, Sir!" and do the best we can. "Slash HR budgets." "Cut HR head count." "Eliminate HR programs." In big companies and small, these have been our marching orders, and always, our response has been "Yes, Sir!" followed by a conscientious effort to carry them out. Time and time again, we take these steps . . . and yet, we know full well that they are shortsighted and potentially destructive to our organization's ultimate mission success.

Now, without a doubt, cooperation and being a good team player are positive attributes for people to have. They help to enhance an organization's efficiency and, as a consequence, its performance. They are the underpinnings of effective management. And that makes them appropriate individual characteristics . . . for peace time. Our world, however, is no longer at peace. That is the change to which we must adapt. Our profession is under attack and so is the American enterprise. We now live in a time of war. And war requires a very different set of attributes, both for soldiers and their leaders.

What makes for success on the organizational chart does not lead to victory on the battlefield. The attributes of career advancement are not the attributes of effective war-fighting. Ironically, that means we must stop playing the role of "good soldiers." We in the HR profession must no longer be the followers of others' orders. We must recast our mission and ourselves. We must see HR anew.

What is our new persona? Who must we become in this relentlessly hostile environment? I believe we must transform ourselves into generals: men and women who lead in combat. We must come to act as they do. We must begin to demonstrate their unique set of attributes, the personal characteristics required to prevail in even the most daunting and difficult of circumstances. We must be leaders who succeed in a time of war.

Being generals—believing in ourselves as front line leaders and adapting ourselves to that role—is no easy task. It requires that we find within ourselves the attributes of great battlefield commanders, that we focus on those attributes and deliberately hone them, and, most importantly, that we act with them in each and every challenge we face. In short, we must transform who we are and what we do, for that is the only way we will fend off the attacks on our profession and gain the high ground in today's and tomorrow's enterprise.

Can we meet this challenge? Do we have what it takes to effect such a change? Those are the most important answers we need . . . and I believe that both can be provided with a single word. Yes.

Peter Weddle
Stamford, CT

What War?

ar. It is not a term or an environment normally associated with Human Resources. Oh sure, HR is always fighting to protect its turf in the internecine battles that are a seemingly intractable part of modern corporate life. But those conflicts—important as they may seem in the push and shove of setting budgets and establishing priorities—are simply skirmishes among ourselves. They are family spats, not battles for existence. They will determine who gets what, at any moment in time, and who is where in the corporate pecking order.

Even as these battles continue, however, we in Human Resources have entered a much more hostile and dangerous time. We have been thrust into the darkness of combat, the tempest of war. Suddenly, our fight has grown more desperate, our conflicts wrought with greater peril. No matter how near or far we are from the actual struggle, the consequences of defeat are now much greater than a smaller budget or a reduced staff. Indeed, this war is a threat to every Human Resource professional, to our occupational security.

Modern wars are much more complex than most people realize, and this war—the war of our time—is no exception. Historically, wars have been fought in theatres or loci of operations. Each theatre is actually a war unto itself with its own unique set of challenges and dangers. Take World War II, for example. It was actually two wars—a War in Europe and a War in Asia and the Pacific. Victory in the European theatre required a carefully tailored campaign of strategies, tactics and resources that was entirely different from the campaign of strategies, tactics and resources required for victory in the Asia-Pacific theatre.

That reality leads to one of the first rules of leadership in a time of war. Victory is possible only if you know what war you are fighting and then devise the right strategies and tactics and accumulate the right resources for that particular conflict. Misperceive your theatre of war or the nature of the required campaign, and defeat will be certain, swift and painful.

So, what war confronts the Human Resource profession? I think it is best described as the field's War for Relevancy. It is a mortal conflict of staggering dimensions which must be waged not in two, but in three concurrent theatres of combat:

- A War for Organizational Security . . . in a time of terror;

- A War for Trust . . . in an era of employee cynicism; and

- A War for the Best Talent . . . in an age of key worker shortages.

THE WAR FOR RELEVANCY

The Human Resource profession is in the fight of its life. A growing chorus of voices—both inside and outside the enterprise—are questioning whether HR skills are a core competency of effective management, whether the HR "function" is a core activity of the modern corporate enterprise. These attacks—for that is what they are—can be found in editorials and op-ed pieces published by business magazines, in the marketing literature of business process outsourcing and consulting companies and in the private conversations of more and more business leaders. If we fail to defend ourselves against these assaults—if we don't do more than try to contain them, if we don't counterattack and defeat them—our collective profession and individual careers are in jeopardy. That is not hyperbole; it is reality.

Why is that so? Because these attacks are very different from what we have experienced in the past. It would be very easy to misperceive them as nothing more than business as usual—the monotonous litany of petty carping about our role in and contribution to the enterprise. They are that, to be sure, but they are also something else more deadly. Today's resource constrained enterprise no longer has the means to support all of its activities. Global competition and a cautious business environment have forced companies to make hard choices among their products and markets and areas of operation. No unit wants to be excluded, of course, so a conflict has erupted to determine which will survive. It is a corporate civil war that pits each and every unit against all other units in the enterprise. The attacks we now face represent the opening shots in that struggle.

For many of us, they have already begun to harm our standing (and hence, our viability) in the enterprise. In late 2002, for example, the Society for Human Resource Management (SHRM) reported the results of a study by the Discovery Group, a consulting firm in Sharon, MA. It polled 425 HR professionals and found that just 48% believe that their profession has the respect of company leaders. Worse, that dismal finding was down from the already agonizingly low figure of 63% in 1995. By our own accounting, therefore, fewer than one-out-of-two organizations are led by those who think HR deserves to be at the leadership table.

Equally as bad, only 54% of the respondents to this survey believe that HR has the decision-making authority it needs to do its job. If you've been in the business world for more than

forty-five minutes, you know that responsibility without
authority is a poison pill. It is the remedy by which an organization expels those elements that are no longer considered
compatible with or useful to its future.

Sadly, there's considerable evidence that many organizations are on the verge of making just such a judgment about
their own HR unit. Consider the following:

- **Talk has become the preferred HR investment in
  today's corporations.** During the go-go days of the
  1990's, every CEO with a public relations advisor clam-
  ored to proclaim the importance of workers and the critical role of HR in marshalling them for success in the
  global marketplace. Human Capital became the mantra of
  the moment in the corner office. And, there it stayed . . .
  until the economy went south. When that happened,
  those grand pronouncements were quickly dumped from
  memory, and company after company reverted to their
  traditional disdain for HR and their minimalist approach
  to supporting it.

  This return to business as usual, however, resulted in
  precious little change for the HR department. Ironically,
  all of the verbal investment CEOs made in Human
  Capital during that overheated period never actually
  translated into greater financial support for the work
  that HR professionals do. Indeed, according to the
  Bureau of National Affairs (BNA), HR department budgets were less than 1% of total annual corporate operating
  costs between 1997 and 2000. In 2003, they were still a
  paltry 0.9% of the total money companies spend to operate their businesses. Such impoverished support is proof
  positive that the perceived value of HR management
  among America's corporate leaders never really went
  up. It was all talk; nothing more. Vapor principles. PR
  posing. Part of the good-time ride of the dot-com bubble.

  And were these leaders called to account for their

empty words? Of course not. Indeed, in most cases, the stock market actually rewarded their talk-not-walk strategy, and in the process, taught a whole generation of corporate leaders that the only investment they need make in HR is lip service. Verbal capital, they discovered, generates a more than sufficient return on asset . . . if, the asset in question is people.

- **What HR does is not what the enterprise needs to do.** In today's difficult business environment, more and more companies are jettisoning any activity not deemed to be a core competency—something that leads directly to creating and sustaining success in the marketplace. These "nonessential" activities must still be performed, however, so they are outsourced to vendors that typically promise cost savings and/or improved customer service. It's an almost irresistible combination: the company gets rid of an operation it doesn't value, and it saves money at the same time.

  Given the low esteem with which HR is held by today's corporate leaders, it should come as no surprise that the function is increasingly viewed as a candidate for what is called BPO—business process outsourcing. According to one estimate by Michael F. Corbett & Associates, Ltd., Human Resource BPO is likely to be a $30-60 billion market. It is very different, however, from traditional HR outsourcing which is typically limited to the execution of discrete administrative tasks (e.g., pay and benefits administration). Indeed, the proponents of and vendors for Human Resource BPO seek to take over virtually all HR functional activity.

  Although we reassure ourselves that this shift is beneficial because it frees us up "to be more strategic" and "to become a business partner" in the organization, the sad reality is something else altogether. There is, of course, absolutely nothing wrong with outsourcing *per se*, but its

use for most or all of HR's key responsibilities begs the
question: why bother with HR at all? The counter argu-
ment by BPO advocates—that the HR department retains
(or somehow magically acquires) strategic oversight of
its work—is self-serving and misguided. If HR is already
weakened from internal attacks and indifference, then the
move to HR BPO is more likely to be its death knell than
its song of liberation. In effect, such broad-gauged outsourcing leaves our profession with an imprecise mission—or, more likely, without any mission whatsoever—in
the enterprise.

These developments frame the theatres of the War for
Relevancy. Each of these theatres provides the opportunity
for us to create a counter force to those who believe that
talk is the preferred HR investment in today's corporation
and that what the HR department does is not what the enterprise needs to do. They are a way for us to go on the offensive and push back those who believe that our profession is
irrelevant. For our actions to be effective, however, we must
have a crystal clear understanding of what's involved in each
theatre. We must be absolutely sure of what war we are fighting in order to devise the appropriate strategies and tactics
and acquire the resources necessary for victory.

What, then, are the dimensions and imperatives of the
three theatres in HR's War for Relevancy?

THE WAR FOR ORGANIZATIONAL SECURITY
. . . IN A TIME OF TERROR

Obviously, the global war against terror—the mortal battle to
protect and preserve American security and way of life—is
far larger than the War for Relevancy facing the Human
Resource profession. The impact of that war on the
American worker, however, is not.

The horrific acts of September 11, 2001 thrust terror into the American workplace. They impaled our comfortable assumption that terrorism is something that happens in distant places and to other people. Today, terrorist acts are real and potent threats to every working person in every American corporation, here at home and around the world. For those of us in the HR profession, they frame the War for Organizational Security.

Terrorism attacks business by depressing our ability to create and sustain economic growth. According to a report by the Employment Policy Foundation, conservative estimates of the heightened security measures in public and private organizations now range between three and five billion dollars annually. That's the equivalent of a 5% "terror tax" on every dollar of Gross Domestic Product in this country. It is a choke hold that strangles day-to-day commerce and undermines our future.

In effect, terrorism endangers both our personal and corporate security, but is it a Human Resource problem? Doesn't it more appropriately belong to the IT Department, the strategic planning group or the corporate security unit? Why is countering terrorism in the workplace a war that HR professionals and their leaders must fight?

There are at least two reasons why we in HR should lead this campaign:

- First, acts of terrorism affect morale and the willingness and ability of employees to give their best on-the-job each day. They prevent people from taking important business trips, from working in tall office buildings, from concentrating on urgent business matters because they are depressed, frightened or worried about their loved ones.

  To address these issues effectively, organizations must have both a well-crafted overall strategy and effective unit-by-unit tactics. While supervisors and business unit managers can and do address unit concerns about terror, only those in the Human Resource profession have the breadth and depth of vision to develop a strategic response to terrorism for a company's entire workforce. They alone have the know-how and corporate-wide perspective to prepare workforce reconstitution plans, to inform employees about those preparations and to ensure that they are practiced and updated, as necessary. Only HR has its finger on workers' collective pulse and thus can establish the right programs to address the anxiety, worry, and fear that undermine morale and optimal performance. In essence, HR is unique in its capacity to preserve and protect the human capital of an enterprise.

- Second, the war against terror also creates special talent management challenges. Not only does the global marketplace virtually dictate that corporations place employees in overseas locations that can now be very dangerous, but national security requirements frequently "undersize" their workforces as employees serve in the National Guard and Reserves. As a consequence, employers must now meet new support and regulatory standards in their treatment of expatriates and accommodations for citizen-soldiers. And, they must do better contingency and workforce planning in order to ensure that corporate operations are neither degraded nor disrupted by hostile events, wherever they may occur around the world.

  Here again, only HR professionals have the knowledge and strategic position in the enterprise to address these challenges on a company-wide basis. They alone have the necessary skills and experience to support overseas employees by providing for their personal and workplace security, by devising and practicing emergency action plans, and by installing Employee Assistance Programs and other benefits to help workers and their families cope with such issues as stress, loneliness and isolation. Similarly, they alone have the know-how and background to address worker shortages by redeploying other employees for optimal company performance, by acquiring contract and temporary workers to fill critical vacancies and by installing job aids to shore up individual work. To put it another way, HR is uniquely positioned to protect expatriates and preserve their contribution to the enterprise and to support the citizen-soldiers of that enterprise as they serve to protect and preserve the American way of life.

Sadly, this time of terror is unlikely to be short-lived, so the War for Organizational Security will be a key corporate concern for some time to come. Our ability to help the enterprise survive and prosper in that environment will, as a consequence, greatly advance our campaign to win the War for Relevancy. It proves that what we do is critical to our organizations and a fulsome return on any real investment made in our work.

THE WAR FOR TRUST . . .
IN AN ERA OF EMPLOYEE CYNICISM

Even as Americans have been forced to deal with the external threat of terrorism, they have also had to endure an onslaught of misdeeds by leaders within their own workplace. Evening after evening, they have been forced to sit through news reports of falsified records, financial chicanery and breathtaking arrogance. They have had to struggle with the decline in their economic well-being, while corporate chieftains brazenly pocketed huge bonuses and stock grants. And, they have had to worry about their own employment security, even as they watched executives ride gilded parachutes safely out of the collapsing enterprises they led.

This bombardment of exposed corporate mismanagement and greed has had two negative consequences in the enterprise:

- A Watson Wyatt survey of nearly 13,000 workers in all professions, crafts and trades, across all industries and at all levels of seniority has found that fewer than two-out-of-five employees, today, have trust or confidence in their senior executives. The fragile bond between leader and led has been ripped and almost severed by too many images of senior executives being led away in handcuffs. And it is that bond—not the public relations savvy of corporate leaders who transfix Wall Street analysts—that breeds sacrifice, superior work and commitment among employees. Those who see their leaders out only for themselves have no model for serving the best interests of the enterprise or any reason to do so. In effect, the devotion to service that creates high performing organizations is the first casualty of mistrust.

- Equally as important, this tattered bond has undermined the financial foundation of employee-investors, retirees and the general public who buy stock in America's companies. According to a Work USA 2002 survey, also conducted by Watson Wyatt, the three year total return to shareholders is almost three times lower at companies where trust has been wounded. In addition, such weakened trust also has a debilitating effect on the economy at large. As some corporate leaders pranced their ill-gotten wealth in public, millions of Americans found themselves out of work, with battered retirement savings accounts, reduced standards of living and, worst of all, the creeping suspicion that the American Dream was lost, not only for themselves, but for their children and grandchildren, as well. That sense of diminished prospects has forced a growing number of people to reduce spending and curtail investments. Their consumer decisions, in turn, have driven down corporate sales and profitability, completing a vicious circle of economic malaise.

Trust has been lost, and trust must be regained before any substantial, sustained economic growth can occur. Who, however, among an enterprise's leaders can wage the war to re-earn the trust of America's workers? Who has the requisite moral standing, organizational breadth of vision, proximity to the workforce and skills to lead a campaign that will win back employee confidence and respect?

Ultimately, of course, the War for Trust is the responsibility of Chief Executive Officers. They have both the stature and the expertise to achieve victory. In many organizations, however, CEOs lack the required proximity to workers and, in some—at least according to the Watson survey—they have lost the moral standing to direct this effort personally. As a result, the enterprise and its CEO now need a field general to lead the action on the battlefield for trust.

In times past, that leader would often have been the Chief Financial Officer, but not today. At this point, such an assignment would likely produce a corporate mutiny. As unfair as it may be, the reputation and credibility of CFOs have been severely harmed by the crimes of their colleagues. Obviously, the vast majority of CFOs are honest, and obviously, they have the capacity—the skills and knowledge—to solve the trust problem. Equally as obvious, however, is the perception by many employees that they are a part of the problem. From employees' perspective, they are damaged leaders and, therefore, not fit to lead the War for Trust.

If not the CFO, then what about one of the other leaders in the enterprise? Can this critical battlefield command be given to another c-level executive—the Chief Information Officer, for example—or to a senior business unit manager? No, it cannot. The functional or line focus of their responsibilities has precluded them from acquiring the company-wide breadth of vision and/or the requisite skills to prosecute such a war. In essence, they have the stature, but not the know-how to do the job. Certainly, they can address the issue of trust within their respective units, but they lack the experience and preparation necessary to implement a campaign for the entire corporation. They are not part of the problem, but they aren't the source of its solution either.

So, who can take on this critical mission? Who has all of what it takes to wage the War for Trust successfully? Clearly, it's the Vice President of Human Resources. Only he or she has the necessary moral authority and expertise to win back employee trust. Indeed, according to the Work USA study cited earlier, employees already make that connection. In companies where they see HR effectively engaged in enterprise leadership, 62% of employees also believe the organization is trustworthy. Conversely, in companies where employees sense that HR is not able to play a leadership role, only 8% believe that the organization's management can be trusted.

Volunteering for—no, aggressively seeking—the leadership role in the War for Trust and then winning that campaign will significantly fortify the position of HR in its War for Relevancy. Moreover, it is an initiative for which no "business case" need be made. Its critical importance is intuitively obvious to the CEO, and to the CFO and every other leader in the enterprise. In taking command, therefore, HR leaders are assigning themselves and their profession a dangerous, but critical mission, and victory there is relevance in action.

THE WAR FOR THE BEST TALENT . . . IN AN AGE OF KEY WORKER SHORTAGES

Talent. There's no more critical resource in the enterprise, and unfortunately, it is always in short supply. Indeed, from an employer's perspective, shortages of key workers—"A" level performers and those with scarce skills—are constant and critical. There is simply never enough of the best and hardest to find.

Even as resumes pour into recruiter e-mailboxes, therefore, employers continue to battle for top talent. Even in a slow growth economy, a War for Talent is still being waged among American employers. It is, however, a very different challenge from the fight for talent in the late 1990's.

During that earlier period, an extraordinary economic expansion coincided with the leading edge of a long-term decline in the size of the American workforce. That combination of trends created a quantitative shortfall in workers, and it, in turn, ignited a fierce battle for new hires among employers. This conflict can best be described as a War for Any Talent. Recruiters were charged with filling so many open positions from such a small candidate pool in the face of such stiff competition that they were often forced to take the first person they found who was qualified and, happily, also had a pulse. Undoubtedly, they would have preferred to search for the single, best candidate for an opening, but there simply wasn't the time or the HR staff available to do so.

When the recession of 2001 cut business activity and diminished the impact of the demographic shift to a smaller workforce, many organizations cut their staffing units and budgets in the mistaken belief that the War for Talent had ended. In fact, of course, it had not. Qualitative constraints—shortages among key workers—never go away. Hence, the War for Any Talent morphed into a War for the Best Talent. It was a shift of tectonic proportions for the staffing component of the HR profession, and it was driven by the force of two key notions about what constitutes a quality worker:

- **A quality worker is someone who has a rare skill in a critical occupational field.** Although there are now large numbers of people looking for work, there are still too few qualified prospects in many key skill areas. For example, according to the Information Technology Association of America (ITAA), the U.S. economy—despite its slow recovery from the recession—created 1.1

million new jobs in the information technology field between 2002 and 2003. The association estimated, however, that as many as 500,000 of these openings went unfilled because IT job seekers did not have the skills that employers needed. Similarly, the National Manufacturing Association surveyed the hard-hit manufacturing sector of the U.S. economy and found that 40% of the employers in that sector are now reporting "severe shortages" in machinists, and 20% are reporting such shortages among engineers.

- **A quality worker is also the rare person who performs at an extremely high level of capability.** The first McKinsey & Company report entitled *The War for Talent*, released in 1997, presented a clear and compelling case for the economic value of top talent. It concluded that "A" level performers are 50-100% more productive than "C" level performers. That finding is true whether the measure of merit is the number of sales closed, the number of products manufactured with zero defects or customer satisfaction scores. In other words, the enterprise with the most top talent has a real and powerful competitive advantage in its markets. No less important— and a rare situation in HR management—that advantage can be measured and monetized. Indeed, the more vacancies an organization fills with the best talent (rather than any talent), the better its financial performance, both in top line revenue and bottom line profitability.

In essence, the War for the Best Talent is a conflict fought on two different, but related battlefields. On one, the goal is to avoid the performance penalty an organization pays when its critical skill positions go unfilled. That penalty includes all of the sales that are not made, the product and service deadlines that are missed, and the blow to employee morale and productivity that comes from asking too much of too few. On the other battlefield, the goal is to capture the performance premium that is provided by "A" level employees. That premium includes the productivity that is gained, the excellence that is achieved, and the pride that is felt by all who work with and for top talent.

While hiring managers clearly play a role in the recruitment process, only the Human Resource department is staffed and trained to wage a War for the Best Talent. It alone knows where to source quality candidates and how to sell them on the value proposition of a job with a specific employer. Only it understands what factors in an organization's employment brand are most important to top prospects and how to communicate that information to them. And, only it has the sense of urgency and the skills necessary to assess and select those applicants who will make the greatest contribution to the advancement of the enterprise.

To date, however, the recruitment campaigns of most HR departments have been less than fully successful . . . at least that's the view of their customers. According to a 2003 survey of corporate executives conducted by the consulting firm Accenture, just 25% of the respondents—a sample of 200 CEOs, COOs, CFOs and CIOs—think that their current employees have the skills to perform at industry-leading levels. Why such unimpressive results? Because the HR department has been forced to wage this war with inadequate resources and priority. In many organizations, short-sighted budget and staff cuts—directed by some of the same executives who were critical of their workers' capabilities—have left these units unable to perform their recruiting mission in the present or to prepare themselves for the inevitable expansion of their responsibilities as the economy strengthens. Sadly, however, we in HR have exacerbated this situation at times by focusing our efforts on process administration and worrying more about procedural purity than our organization's strategic objectives in employment. The net result is the large and growing number of employers that are now drowning in resumes and still hiring other than the best talent for their missions.

These are real obstacles, to be sure, but they can and must be overcome. HR professionals and their leaders must rise to the challenge and guide their organizations to victory in the War for the Best Talent. That outcome, and only that outcome, will enable their employers to achieve their corporate mission. They cannot take the high ground in either the domestic or global marketplace with advanced technology or even with the tactical brilliance of business unit leaders. Important as those two assets are, their value to the enterprise depends entirely on the unique advantage of high caliber employees with state-of-the-art skills. Recruit them, and the HR department will dramatically enhance its organization's economic position, and, as a result, forcefully advance its own cause in the War for Relevancy.

WHAT CONSTITUTES VICTORY?

The War for Relevancy, then, is a complex engagement consisting of three great challenges. How will we know when victory has been achieved? We will see Human Resource Management firmly established as an integral and primary activity of the modern enterprise—a function that is not only core to its operations, but also, essential to its success in the marketplace and the market. Winning the War for Relevancy will, for the first time, provide all of the justification necessary for sustained, meaningful investment in HR programs and activities. Our victory will not make us strategic partners; it will make us something far more important: strategic leaders—men and women who can help guide their organizations forward in the face of even the most daunting challenges.

These advances, however, are conditional. They are not a new right we have acquired, but a new responsibility we must accept. Victory does not mean we are done with our fight, but rather, that we have successfully embarked on a new mission, a mission to be the change we want to see in our profession. Moreover, our progress will quickly stop, if we revert to old behaviors and allow ourselves to be lulled back into old roles. In a word, then, victory in the War for Relevancy is opportunity; it is our chance to make a difference, to have the real and vital impact we have always sought in the organizations for which we work.

That definition, in turn, transforms our victory from something that simply benefits HR into an achievement that serves the well being of the enterprise, itself. In taking this stand, we acknowledge that it is our job to defend and enhance the success of our employers. By fighting these battles, we engage ourselves in the front line business of those organizations. By winning the War—our War for Relevancy—we reinforce their performance and advance the value they provide to shareholders and stakeholders alike. That is our ultimate objective and the essential character of our victory.

HOW DO WE WIN THESE WARS?

Fighting one war and winning is an enormous challenge. Fighting three wars at the same time and winning all of them is a monumental undertaking. And yet, to do less poses huge risks to each and all of us in the Human Resource profession. We must fight and fight both to lead and win on every battlefield because that is the only way to prevail in the War for Relevancy. And, we must achieve a full and unconditional victory in this War because that is the only way to secure the special mission of our calling, to make all of the contribution to the enterprise that we can and must.

But, how do we wage and win these wars? Most of us are unfamiliar with the imposing conditions and heavy demands of battle. Very few of us have had the experience or training required to lead a military campaign. So, while it's clear that we must do something different—that what has served us well in times of peace will not suffice in a time of war—we don't know how to proceed. What will cause our success on these unfriendly fields of strife? Where can we turn to uncover the essential elements of effective war fighting? How can we achieve our victory?

The answers to those questions can be found in the study of military art or, more precisely, in a special subset of that discipline: the individual characteristics of successful combat generals. Their unique qualities forge victory in the most demanding and perilous of human endeavors. Their essential attributes are what it takes to win at war. Collectively, these traits are known as Generalship.

Generalship

A very small percentage of Americans, today, have had any experience in or even any contact with the military. As a consequence, generals are often unknown figures, seen perhaps on the evening news or quoted in a newspaper article. And what generals do, by extension, is also often unclear. We know they are the leaders of the military. Most of us understand that they are men and women who have been especially trained to bear the heavy responsibility of leading others—our mothers and fathers, brothers and sisters, sons and daughters—into combat in times of war. But what is it that makes a general a general? And, why should HR professionals and their leaders study them?

The first of those two questions is important only after the second has been addressed. So, what does being a general have to do with being a successful HR professional and leader?

- **This is a time of war, not peace for the HR profession.** Clearly, the answer begins with the environment in which we find ourselves today: the War for Relevancy and its constituent theatres of combat. Conventional HR responsibilities will undoubtedly continue unabated, but all around us—encroaching on our responsibilities and our work—there are real and pressing threats. It is not exaggeration to say, therefore, that HR is now fighting for its future.

We must win this conflict or risk fading into irrelevancy and, ultimately, extinction in the modern enterprise. And, winning it will involve the successful, simultaneous prosecution of campaigns in three very different theatres: the War for Organizational Security, the War for Trust, and the War for the Best Talent. These challenges are urgent; they are momentous; and they are perilous to each and all of us, personally and professionally. Only those who prepare—who recognize and acquire the critical elements of victory—will survive and prevail.

Such preparation is the unique province of generals. Of all the various kinds of leaders found in modern society, only generals are trained explicitly for times of conflict, pressure and crisis . . . for the grave accountabilities and outsized challenges of leadership in a time of war. Certainly, there are superlative peace time generals, but few are remembered. The generals we celebrate, the ones we study as great leaders—Grant, Lee, Pershing, Patton, MacArthur, Bradley, Powell, Franks—they were all war time generals. Successful in peace, to be sure, but renowned as exemplars of victorious leadership in war.

- **Human Resource leaders are now generals, not managers.** The War for Organizational Security, the War for Trust and the War for the Best Talent have thrust upon the Human Resource profession and its leaders a critical new role in the modern enterprise. Collectively, these enormous challenges charge HR executives with the heavy responsibility of directing human capital formation in the enterprise. In a service-based, global economy, the value of an organization's human capital and the organization's ability to extract that value and put it to work spells the difference between victory and defeat. And, the value of human capital is determined by its readiness to work in uncertain times, its faith in corporate leaders, and its skills and level of performance.

Of all the activity centers in the enterprise, HR is best positioned to lead this campaign to optimize human capital formation. With the sole exception of the War for the Best Talent, however, the profession did not consciously seek such a role. This is not a power grab in the corporate headquarters. It is not some unseemly maneuver for personal aggrandizement. No, this assignment—for that is what it is, in essence—recognizes what has happened all around us. The confluence of events outside the HR profession—from terrorist attacks and corporate scandals to demographic trends—brought this challenge to HR. And felicitously, the profession has the individual and collective capacity to respond. As previously noted, only HR possesses the unsullied reputation, the corporate-wide breadth of vision and the array of skills necessary to address these issues effectively. That may sound uncomfortably like chest-beating, but it's not. It is simply a statement of fact.

Our acceptance of that fact—and more importantly, our acceptance of this leadership assignment—will transform Human Resource Management from a nice-to-have activity to a mission critical operation. It will fundamentally change what we do . . . from the supervision of an overhead function to the line responsibility of marshalling an organization's human power in the accomplishment of its mission. And, it will transfigure the HR executive from a peace time manager to a war time general.

This re-imagination of the HR profession—this new war time leadership role in the American enterprise—gives meaning to the other question posed earlier. Now, it makes sense. Indeed, now, we must know the answer if we are to survive and succeed. What is it that makes generals effective war time leaders? What is the essence—what are the critical elements—of their leadership? What guides and shapes it? What is generalship?

GENERALSHIP: THE CRITICAL ELEMENTS OF VICTORY

Webster's Dictionary defines generalship as "military skill in a high commander." That skill encompasses both the development and the implementation of strategy and tactics in support of a unit's mission. The strategy and tactics, in turn, are the general's plans for applying people, technology and resources to secure objectives and the execution of those plans on a day-to-day, hour-by-hour basis. In essence, then, generalship is how a leader envisions operations and makes them happen.

Those who have dedicated their life's work to studying generals, however, would likely hold that the key factor separating the most successful war time generals from all others is something very different from functional expertise. Important as that military skill is—indeed, it is the precondition for success on the battlefield—strategic and tactical competence, in and of itself, is insufficient to achieve victory. There is yet another factor that is absolutely critical to effective war time leadership. That factor is the nexus of attributes that define the person. Military skill is the essential foundation of generalship, but individual traits—a leader's personal characteristics—are what make a good general a great one. They determine how the general's skill is applied—its timing, point of application, duration and specific nature—and thus fundamentally shape the course and ultimate outcome of the battle.

What are these personal characteristics? Time and time again, the battlefield performance of the most effective generals reveals that they are:

- **Courageous** . . . *willing to be at the tip of the spear*
  Successful war time generals do not hold back behind the line. Instead, they put themselves at the leading edge of the battle and at its most decisive point, where the right decisions and actions will lead to victory.

- **Focused** . . . *clear-sighted despite the fog of battle*
  The best war time generals fix their attention on a single issue: the successful prosecution of the battle. As a consequence, they are able to see through the multitude of clamorous distractions, competing priorities and dead ends to identify exactly what must be done to carry the day.

- **Selfless** . . . *possessing the soul of a warrior*
  Great war time generals believe they must model the personal sacrifice and the devotion to one's fellow soldiers that are the building blocks of victory. They do so in the hand-to-hand fighting on the battlefield and in the urban combat of public opinion, regardless of the consequences to their own well-being and stature.

- **Humble** . . . *always a companion in the foxhole*
  The most effective war time generals recognize their own limitations and compensate for them by surrounding themselves with those who have the skills they lack. They are formidable at building internal teams and, if necessary, external coalitions to achieve the critical mass of power required for mission success.

- **Bold** . . . *imbued with the spirit of the bayonet*
  War time generals know that victory is only achieved by decisive action, never by holding the line, defending in place or hunkering down. They recognize that their actions must be carefully calculated and well planned, but they also understand and accept that these initiatives, by their very nature, always have a measure of risk. And still, they act.

- **Resilient** . . . *unmoved by the shocks of combat*
  Great generals are tenacious in their pursuit of victory.
  They will not be deterred by setbacks or difficulties.
  They know that important battles cannot be won without facing down such challenges, so they prepare for the
  hardships and train those around them to have the
  strength to prevail.

- **Inspirational** . . . *seasoned with a feel for the troops*
  War time generals are not distant leaders. They place
  themselves among those whom they lead and work
  shoulder-to-shoulder with them, sharing adversity as
  well as achievement, hardships as well as victory.
  Through this bond of shared experience, great generals
  come to know what they must do to draw out the best
  of their subordinates, even in the most difficult of circumstances.

All generals have these seven attributes to some
degree, but great war time generals seem to have a deeper,
richer store of them. Does that make them perfect? Are
great war time generals exemplars of what one military
writer has described as "the piety of Saint Paul, the intel-
lect of Albert Einstein, and the courage of Joan of Arc?" Of
course not. Generals—even great generals—miscalculate
and make mistakes just as other leaders do. Generals are
sometimes forced to retreat in order to fight and win
another day. And, in certain situations, despite their attributes and skill, the circumstances of a battle deny them any
way of winning. Indeed, for every general who leads his
unit to victory, there is at least another who has failed.
That is the nature of combat.

These attributes, however, are the essential elements of
victory in a time of war. While they are not a guarantee of
success—for nothing in the real world ever is—they, at least,
make it possible and significantly improve its odds. What is

certain, on the other hand, is that no general has ever pre-vailed on the battlefield without a fulsome measure of these traits. They are, then, the essence—the marrow—of great leadership in difficult times.

WHAT MUST HR LEADERS & PROFESSIONALS DO?

HR leaders and those who aspire to be cannot ignore the War for Relevancy. We did not ask for this conflict, but now that it's here, we have no choice but to fight. In fact, ignor-ing the war—pretending that it does not exist or hoping that it will somehow go away—is the one sure strategy for defeat. Further, if we are going to fight, then surely, we must fight to win. As one of America's most famous war time generals, Douglas MacArthur, once said, "There is no substitute for vic-tory." And, the only way to achieve our victory—the only way to protect and preserve our profession—is to arm our-selves with the attributes of great war time generals.

Now, some will argue that such traits are unique gifts—a special alignment of the stars that occurs in only a small num-ber of people—and only they have the potential to be great leaders. There are others, however—from Thomas Jefferson who established West Point in 1802 to military scholars study-ing the leadership of generals on today's battlefields—who believe that each person has, within them, the attributes of effective leadership in difficult times. This book strongly sides with the latter school of thought. We—all of us, every single member of the Human Resource profession—have the poten-tial to be a general, to be a leader in a time of war.

In most of us, however, the attributes of generalship have lain dormant. There has not been the compelling need or the genuine opportunity to exercise them. No crisis has existed; no threat has loomed large. We have, by and large, had the good fortune to live and work in a time of peace.

That, of course, is no longer the case. Our reality has changed. We now face battles we cannot avoid or fail to win. And we must, as a consequence, find and awaken the traits of generalship within us. We must nurture and practice them, stretch and strengthen them. "We must," as Gandhi once said, "be the change we wish to see in the world." We must be the leaders that our enterprises need.

The following chapters provide a roadmap for that campaign. They recount the actions of great generals on the battlefield and the lessons we can learn from their leadership. They illustrate how victory is won by the application of professional skill and knowledge and, most importantly, by the special power of generalship—the individual attributes of the leader.

Courageous

Willing to Be At the Tip of the Spear

A war time general wants to be, needs to be—insists on being—where the action is. Not just any action, but the most critical action. The decisive spot on the battlefield. The tipping point of greatest danger and consequence. The forward edge of operations, where success or failure will be determined, where victory will be won or lost.

In the military, this attribute is called being "at the tip of the spear." Not in the corner office or some comfortable cubicle, not in the headquarters building, but in the field with the units that are doing the fighting or the work. General Montgomery C. Meigs once described it this way to a group of officers who had just been promoted to the rank of general:

> "Get out from under the pressure of the calendar and focus on the human element of the organization."

He was rightly saying that, all too often, leaders let appointments and meetings, memo-writing and staff sessions prevent them from being in touch with the men and women who work in their organizations. They somehow forget that their role is, by definition, to work with other people; they are specifically charged with motivating, organizing and directing them in the accomplishment of a mission. And, in difficult times, especially in difficult times, that cannot be done—at least, it cannot be done effectively—from afar, from the safety and security of distant places. Leadership in war can only be performed successfully in the midst of its human element—at the tip of the spear.

This attribute, however, involves more than simple geography. It also includes what the leader does when he or she is present at the tip of the spear. Great generals don't place themselves at the front to observe, but to lead. To learn, by first hand experience, what is actually happening. And then, to apply that knowledge to craft and supervise battle plans that are appropriate for the reality of the situation. To see and be seen and to determine the outcome of events.

The actions of General Matthew Ridgeway offer an illustrative example. He once wrote, "A basic element in troop leadership is the responsibility of the commander to be where the crisis of action is going to happen." Only by being at that location of imminent import can the leader know what to do to turn the tide of the battle in his or her unit's favor and take those steps necessary to achieve that advantage.

But Ridgeway did more than write about being at the tip of the spear. He practiced courage in his own leadership. During the darkest days of the Korean War, he assumed command of the main American force on the battlefield, the United States Eighth Army. The unit was reeling back under the pressure of the Chinese Army's massive attack into South Korea. Burned-out vehicles and the wounded clogged the main highway as fresh troops moved forward into the battle line. Even with reinforcements, however, the situation remained desperate. Morale plummeted; fear began to spread. So, what did Ridgeway do? Within 48 hours of taking command, he moved his headquarters forward, as well, right up to the edge of the battle.

Once he got there, he didn't sit still. He visited every unit, every corps and every division. It was the dead of winter, cannon fire thundered just ahead, and still he went. He walked the battlefield, talking with soldiers and their commanders, instilling confidence, reviewing and, if necessary, changing tactics, and ensuring that his troops had the resources they needed for victory. In the words of one of his subordinates:

> "He breathed humanity into the operation. He got their spirits up, he saw the solders were warm, properly fed, properly led. Sure, a few people had to go. They were good people, most of them, but they were tired, they had been in that war too long, they were worn out. . . . He kept the spirit of the offensive. . . ."

As General Ridgeway demonstrated, being at the tip of the spear involves active, forceful leadership from the head of the line, the front of the unit. There is, of course, little or no cover out there; policies and procedures, rule books and headquarters directives don't have much sway in the face of real and hard challenges and what must be done to meet them successfully. At the tip of the spear, the imperative is making right decisions so that right actions can be taken. It is all about saying no, when no is the right answer. And saying yes, even when it is dangerous or difficult to do so.

It takes courage to assume such a position, to be up close to the battle and to place one's own safety at risk in order to ferret out and execute the course that will carry the day. And, that's why the other purpose of being at the tip of the spear is to rally one's subordinates. To instill bravery by modeling it. To stir sacrifice from others by showing one's own unwavering determination. To pull the best out of those whom one leads by demonstrating the best a leader can offer—to share the danger and adversity, and yet, rise above it. To signal the way to victory.

How does this concept apply to HR professionals and their leaders? In several ways:

- First, being courageous means identifying the point where "the crisis of action is going to happen" in the War for Organizational Security, the War for Trust and the War for the Best Talent. For example, Human Resources Forum 2003, an annual gathering of senior HR professionals, concluded that one such turning point in the War for Trust will be the oversight of corporate legal and ethical standards. That cannot be accomplished, of course, by observation from distant headquarters or by passive investigation from the safety of one's office. It can only be done by active reconnoitering at the front lines, in the operating units.

- Second, being courageous involves using the vantage point at the tip of the spear to determine what will be required to turn the tide of battle toward victory. According to the Forum survey, 79% of the HR executives who responded said they would report violations by their company to proper authorities; and 83% said they would take "strong action" whenever they learned of legal or ethical violations. They would not simply observe, but instead, find a way to influence the outcome of the war.

- And third, being courageous means leading one's unit in the implementation of that plan, in taking the decisive action required for victory. The Forum asked over 300 HR executives for their observations, and a January, 2003 article in *HRMagazine* described its final report.

  " . . . the report concludes that HR leaders are in a strong position to keep corporate malfeasance in check and that they will put their jobs on the line if necessary to enforce legal and ethical standards."

That's leadership at the tip of the spear. That's modeling the courage that will win the War for Trust.

It is also all of the justification that's required to change the composition of corporate Boards of Directors. These bodies, charged as they are with corporate governance, represent a key battleground in the War for Trust. For that reason, every Board of every corporation, public and private, should now have a Vice President of Human Resources (VP/HR) among its members. However, that individual should not be the VP/HR of the organization the Board oversees—inevitably, that would create the perception, if not the reality, of a conflict of interest. Instead, the Board member should be the VP/HR of another, peer organization, and he or she should automatically be appointed to the Board's Compensation Committee and its Ethics Committee, should one exist. In this way, the Board equips itself to serve the corporation in its War for Trust and publicly communicates its intention to do so. Hence, senior HR executives should now be among the most intensely recruited and prized members of America's corporate Board of Directors, a position that's indisputably at the tip of the spear in today's climate of shareholder activism.

But, isn't assuming such a visible position risky or even dangerous? Of course, it is. At the tip of the spear, the leader is fully exposed. You are out front and in the open, where there is no ducking responsibility. Where everyone can see you and your actions. Where the outcome—good or bad—isn't known, but will turn on what you do.

Take General Thomas J. "Stonewall" Jackson. He earned his nickname at the First Battle of Bull Run in the Civil War. His troops were wavering in the face of a ferocious Union attack. Rifle fire swept over the ranks like a billowing curtain of steel; cannon shot sprayed into the huddled groups of men. Just as the line was about to buckle, a soldier looked up and saw Jackson astride his horse right at the forward line of the battle. The Union assault rose to a fever pitch, but still, Jackson held his ground. His resolve and courage revived the flagging spirits of his troops. They rallied, counterattacked and carried the day.

A year later, that same determination to be at the tip of the spear made General Jackson a casualty of war. It was the Battle of Chancellorsville, and once again, he was right in the midst of the fight. This time, however, he was out in front of his lines at night, reconnoitering the enemy. There was no moonlight, the shadows held danger, and the sentries were edgy. As he spurred his horse back through the trees to his own positions, he was mistaken for one of the enemy by his own troops. A fusillade of shot rang out, and General Jackson was hit. He would later die of complications from his wounds.

For HR leaders, of course, the danger is not mortal, but it is very real. It can harm their standing in the organization or worse, maim their career. And just as bad, the threat is as likely to come from behind as it is to come from the tip of the spear. Why? Because the closer to the action a leader gets, the further he or she must necessarily be from the headquarters and rear echelon commanders. That absence, in turn, creates a vacuum with two potentially harmful consequences:

- The first, predictably, is the threat to their own position and stature, as intrigue and simple proximity shift the balance of power among competing interests. HR leaders must guard their rear flank—they must attend to their position and influence in the headquarters—even as they lead from the front. To put it another way, they cannot prevail on the battlefield without a firm foundation of support behind them.

- The second threat is that of interference by those who are not on the front lines. If these rear echelon commanders occupy positions of power, they can make decisions and issue directives that degrade or even disrupt the successful prosecution of the battle. The U.S. military has long upheld the principle that the "commander on the ground" always has the most accurate understanding of

the situation and thus must have the last and final decision when it comes to leading the fight. When that
maxim is ignored, the leader faces a threat that can be
every bit as real as an attack by the enemy.

Take the case of General Zachary Taylor. In 1845, he was
dispatched to Texas to mobilize and train an army to prevent
the continued northward expansion of Mexico, an offensive
that had already cost Americans dearly at the Battle of the
Alamo. He had only partially completed that assignment
when a series of raids north of the border by the Mexican
army caused President James K. Polk to order Taylor to move
on the city of Monterrey, in the interior of Mexico. The general cobbled together a force, marched them deep into the
heart of enemy territory and began his assault. After fierce
fighting in a three-day battle, the Mexican army asked to surrender, and Taylor, whose own forces were down to the last
of their ammunition, agreed. He announced an eight-week
armistice, subject to the approval of both governments, and
permitted the Mexican forces to withdraw with their colors
and honor intact.

Unfortunately, Taylor's decision—an entirely responsible
course of action given the military situation at the tip of the
spear—did not play well back in the nation's capital.
President Polk worried that the cessation of hostilities would
undermine his policy of Manifest Destiny in the Mexican-
contested areas of California and New Mexico and, no less
important, that the swift and victorious conclusion of hostilities would elevate Taylor to a potential contender in the
upcoming Presidential elections. As a consequence, the
President rejected the armistice, and ordered the fighting
resumed.

To implement his decision, Polk directed Taylor to march
on Mexico City, a campaign that would take the general's
battle-weary troops even further into enemy territory and

across several hundred miles of desert. From his vantage point at the tip of the spear, Taylor knew that such a move would endanger his army and virtually guarantee its defeat. He refused to carry out the order, arguing instead that a strike against the Mexican capital was best launched from Vera Cruz, a city on the eastern coast of the country. It was a strategy that would later be vindicated on the battlefield.

Nevertheless, in taking this step, Taylor clearly placed his own career in jeopardy. As the on-site commander, he believed that he knew what was best for his unit and would not be dissuaded from that course of action. The President, however, was infuriated by this act of insubordination and considered relieving Taylor of his command. Luckily, General Winfield Scott, the Army's commanding general, was appropriately supportive of his subordinate and interceded on his behalf. Taylor was permitted to remain with his troops and, shortly thereafter, achieved one of the greatest combat victories in the history of the U.S. Army.

Just outside the little town of Buena Vista, not far from Monterrey, the American force was attacked by a Mexican army that outnumbered it five-to-one. As the battle unfolded, the American line was breached in several places and hand-to-hand fighting ensued. Right in the middle of the din and roar of the guns was General Taylor. As one historian wrote, "There was Zachary Taylor, sitting sideways on his horse, unperturbed under point-blank musketry fire, calmly ordering . . . 'Double shot your guns and give 'em Hell!'" The troops followed his lead and stood their ground. His courage stirred their courage, and despite desperate odds, they carried the day.

Zachary Taylor led from the tip of the spear. He was courageous in the face of battlefield danger and the risk posed by rear echelon interference. Why should HR leaders and professionals do the same? Because being at the tip of the spear is the only place where they too can truly influence the action. It is the one location where they can put their mark on the course of events and inspire those whom they lead to follow them to victory. It is the singular spot on the battlefield where they can demonstrate the courage of a great combat general—a leader in a time of war—and have it make a difference.

WHAT MUST HR LEADERS & PROFESSIONALS DO?

 Determine the issue, the location, the situation that represents "where the crisis of action is going to happen" in each of the theatres in your organization. What are the decisive points where victory or defeat will be determined in your employer's War for Organizational Security, War for Trust and War for the Best Talent? Then, as events unfold, continuously review your selections to ensure that they remain the key points of leverage in each of the theatres.

Evaluate alternative courses of action that you can take at each of the points of crisis. What can you do and what are the risks and potential benefits of doing so? What are the dangers looming behind you and what options do you have to control or defuse them? Wherever possible, select plans that both maximize your probability of success in each theatre and minimize the likelihood of rear area interference. If achieving both objectives is not possible, always follow the course that will optimize your performance and decide the outcome at the tip of the spear.

 Place yourself at the tip of the spear. Be out in front of your unit, leading it in the implementation of your battle plans. Forget about doing more with less; instead, do more with courage. Show your colleagues and your adversaries that you have the conviction and the fortitude to do what it takes to win.

Focused

Clear-Sighted Despite the Fog of Battle

The fog of battle is a legendary aspect of combat. It is the metaphorical and often very real cloud of darkness that descends over a battlefield as the situation grows increasingly complex. It is a fitting description of the diminished visibility or situational awareness that occurs with the actions of numerous, different people and groups; rapidly changing circumstances, both planned and unplanned; and the imprecision of intelligence gathered from imperfect vantage points and perceptions. The fog of battle has confused even the most experienced of combat leaders and disrupted even the most brilliant of strategies and tactics.

Great war time generals, however, seem to have a special internal lens that enables them to penetrate the fog and see clearly what is happening. They use that clarity of perception to keep themselves and their units focused on the ultimate objective—victory—and on the steps they must take to achieve that end. They rely on it to assess the situation with precision, to find the key trends, to identify the critical issues and to discern the turning points in rapidly moving and intricate operations. They then build on that assessment to pinpoint accurately the right course of action that will carry the day and communicate that direction unambiguously to their

subordinates so that it can be implemented effectively . . .
even as the chaos of combat swirls around them.

In the routine world of business, traditional operating
scenarios may get hectic from time-to-time, but they seldom
resemble the rapid-fire pace, shifting circumstances or
intense demands of the battlefield. To put it another way, the
peace time environment in modern enterprises does not
generate the fog of battle. An HR leader can see what needs
to be done and plot out a strategy and set of supporting tactics to implement it. He or she has a firm grasp on—a clear
and detailed understanding of—the priorities, the available
resources and the processes and procedures that are to be
followed to accomplish the traditional, long-standing, everyday mission of Human Resources.

That benign environment, unfortunately, is gone. In today's
War for Relevancy, what is happening and what must be done
are much less clear and apparent. The War for Organizational
Security, the War for Trust and the War for the Best Talent have
exploded into a disconcerting whirlwind of rapidly evolving
external pressures and internal debates, familiar and new personalities, recognized and hidden biases, intensified politics
and constant maneuvering, redefined requirements and competing priorities, and increased scrutiny and escalating risk. In
short, HR leaders are now enveloped in the fog of battle . . .
whether they realize it or not.

Clear-sightedness in such an uncertain milieu can only
be achieved by executing four critical steps. The battlefield
actions of General Ulysses S. Grant offer an illustrative case
in point.

General Grant was promoted to the command of a Union
army at the Battle of Shiloh, in the Civil War. He arrived on
the battlefield to find that his unit was already in the fight and
reeling back under a ferocious, surprise attack by
Confederate forces. It was unclear where his combat battal-
ions were and what condition they were in. Worse, his army's
ammunition and other supplies were scattered across the hill-

sides. Confusion reigned, and as the fog thickened, there seemed to be no way of determining exactly what the army could or should do next.

Grant, however, refused to surrender to the situation. He knew that his army risked destruction if he couldn't find a way through the fog. He had to see clearly where others saw only chaos, and with that focus, he had to set a course that would enable his unit to recover. And, the only way to do that, ironically, was to ride into the heart of the battle.

Grant had sprained his ankle on his way to the battlefield, so he had himself propped up on his horse with a crutch lashed to his saddle. He then rode across the hills and farm fields, talking to his subordinate commanders, directing the construction of defensive positions and rallying the flagging morale of his soldiers. After a period of time, he stopped and from his saddle wrote to General Don C. Buell, another Union commander, who was bringing reinforcements down the Tennessee River. His message read:

> "The attack on my forces has been very spirited since early this morning. The appearance of fresh troops in the field now would have a powerful effect both by inspiring our men and disheartening for the enemy. If you can get upon the field, leaving all of your baggage on the east bank of the river, it will be a move to our advantage and possibly save the day to us. The rebel force is estimated at over 100,000 men. My headquarters will be in the log building on top of the hill, where you will be furnished with a staff officer to guide you to your place on the field."

Grant had quickly collected information about his army's situation, organized that information into a clear understanding of the status of the battle at that moment, formulated a course of action to defend and improve his army's position, and described that strategy and its rationale, clearly and succinctly, to his fellow commander. His communiqué had clear directions:

- leave behind unnecessary equipment,

- arrive on the battlefield quickly,

- bolster our troops morale and undermine that of the enemy, and

- meet me to learn where best to apply your forces on the ground.

Buehl, as a consequence, was able to grasp exactly what was asked of him as well as Grant's reasoning behind the plan. He responded by doing just as Grant asked, and the strategy—plotted from a saddle in the midst of battle—worked perfectly. It stabilized the situation long enough for Grant to reorganize his troops and repel the Confederate attack.

Enveloped in crisis, with the fog of battle swirling around him, Grant moved forward to the tip of the spear to apprehend the situation, to see for himself what was actually happening. He then used that information to formulate an effective battle plan and communicated it accurately to those who could implement it successfully. The entire process was executed quickly and with an intensity of purpose that brooked neither interruption nor diversion. Grant pushed aside his own injury and the danger on the battlefield to concentrate on one objective and one objective only: what it would take to win.

Grant's actions provide a roadmap for how war time commanders achieve focus.

- **First, war time leaders collect intelligence.** They move to the tip of the spear to find out exactly what is happening. However, while Grant could survey the entire battlefield in several hours on horseback, modern military leaders often face a much larger and more complex area of operations. Hence, they must talk to as many people as possible and collect as much sensor data as they can (from drones, satellites, electronic eavesdropping and other sources) to assemble a multifaceted portrait of the situation. The goal is not to develop a monochromatic summary of what is going on, but rather to assemble a richly textured mosaic that describes the situation in all of its variability and detail.

For the HR leader, the collection of intelligence is a similar exercise. It involves being with the people who are at that point in the organization "where the crisis of action is going to happen" and talking to them about their perceptions of what has occurred, what is happening at the moment and what is likely to unfold in the relevant future.

It also depends upon the use of metrics—the sensors of the enterprise battlefield—to acquire data that provide an additional perspective on the situation, a view without the potential bias of human observation. HR metrics, however, are often misunderstood. Unlike financial measures, their purpose is not audit, but excellence. Their data can describe the present with accurate measurements of on-going performance and be predictive of the future through trend analysis. In other words, they enable the leader to see backward in time (as in budget reports), forward in time (as in workforce planning forecasts) and at a particular moment in time (as in recruitment status reports). And, that insight is best used to improve the performance of the unit.

Metrics, however, are only as good as their range of application. The intelligence they provide is limited to where they are used on the battlefield. As obvious as that may seem, it is important to acknowledge that metrics cannot provide the leader with intelligence on what they do not measure. Hence, the key to using metrics effectively—including HR metrics—is to embed them as widely into operations as possible, thereby ensuring the most comprehensive depiction of the situation.

For example, in order to have a good understanding of how well the War for the Best Talent is going in their organizations, a growing number of HR leaders are turning to the use of staffing metrics. While that is a positive development, its impact is being degraded because, all too often, the range of metrics deployment is limited to simple measures of efficiency (e.g., cost-per-hire, time-to-fill). Hence, HR leaders are not seeing the full reality of the talent battlefield and thus lack the perspective required to conceptualize the best tactics for total victory.

To gain such a comprehensive view, HR leaders need more widely distributed metrics. Optimally, these "sensors" should collect intelligence in three areas:

- process efficiency or how well the staffing function is using the enterprise resources (e.g., budget, staff time) it's been given—these metrics might include cost-per-hire and time-to-fill;

- the perceived value of the staffing function's contribution to the work of the enterprise—these metrics might include customer satisfaction scores and new hire performance appraisals; and

- how well the staffing function is managing the assets of the enterprise (e.g., the resume database, the corporate career site) that have been assigned to it— these metrics might include fill rates and quality of yield from the talent database and/or recruitment Web-site.

These data hold the key to the only outcome a war time HR leader can and should accept: total performance improvement. All other outcomes simply multiply the risk for HR in its War for the Best Talent.

- **Second, war time leaders turn the intelligence they collect into knowledge.** Great generals create an accurate mental map of what is happening. They integrate the raw intelligence data on the fly—no paralysis by analysis for combat commanders—and reach an accurate understanding of the true nature of the battle. In the military, this process is called fusion: the integration of disparate information into a single, accurate macro-vision of the battlefield.

  The Duke of Marlborough, one of England's most famous war time generals, modeled this intelligence-into-knowledge step against the French army in the 1708 Battle of Oudenarde. In this complex engagement, Marlborough lead an Allied force of Dutch, Prussian and British troops against a French force that moved rapidly across the rolling hills northwest of Flanders in Belgium. Even as he personally directed the placement of troops on his left flank, he accumulated and distilled a flood of reports rushing in from different units in different situations and locations on the battlefield to create one clear vision of the course to victory. One of his subordinate generals described his demeanor this way:

  > ". . . traits of serene comprehensive judgment, serene in disappointment or stress, unbiased by the local event in which he was himself involved, this fixing with untiring eye and absolute selflessness the problem as a whole. . . ."

  How is this accurate mental map compiled? How is a general able to achieve such a sharp focus in the midst of confusion and constant change? War time generals know that the first conclusion developed from the first intelligence is often wrong. Hence, they continuously test hypotheses as new data are acquired and always discipline themselves to avoid quick judgments. In some cases, this step is an exercise in solitary analysis; in others, it involves marshalling the best minds at hand.

For example, during the critical early hours of the D-Day invasion, General Omar Bradley was commanding an American army that found itself pinned down among the interlacing hedgerows of the French countryside. The German Army was conducting serial ambushes from these obstacles, inflicting heavy and rapidly rising casualties on Bradley's desperate forces. He knew that if a way to break out wasn't found quickly, the entire Allied assault could founder.

What did Bradley do? He had a tent pitched on the beach with nothing but a large table inside. On the table, he placed a map that was oriented to correspond with the terrain. Next, he had the map marked with the latest intelligence about the locations of various types of German and American units as well as their strengths, capabilities and status. Then, as cannon fire carrumped in the background, he assembled all of his subordinate commanders and asked them to study the lay of the land and their combat situation. He led them through the development of a collective mental map of the problem and from it, the construction of a revised concept of operations. That new strategy, based on an up-to-the-minute vision of the battlefield, enabled Bradley's army to break out from the hedgerows and restart the advance of the Allied attack.

A similar process can be used in HR. For example, an organization that is using metrics in its War for the Best Talent may, at some point, acquire data indicating that its candidate quality is declining. However, those data do not provide the knowledge necessary to generate a solution to the problem. Data is transformed into knowledge only through analysis, an assessment of the validity and meaning of the data and, equally as important, an investigation of what is causing the data to be what they are.

To perform that analysis, the HR department might then assemble a Bradley-like meeting to hear the views of recruiters, new hires, candidates and hiring managers. An effective war time leader, however, will not let such a meeting descend into parochial charges and counter charges. Bradley, for example, knew that he had to encourage openness and candor without losing control. Because each unit's problems were having a cascading effect on other units and thus degrading their performance as well, his meeting could easily have dissolved into backbiting and recriminations. Therefore, he kept the participants focused on fixing the problem, rather than on fixing the blame.

The HR leader must do the same. He or she must demand that the participants in a problem-solving meeting focus not on what's wrong, but on how to make it right; not on how bad the situation is, but on how to make it better. Hence, they must adhere to both:

- a neutrality of perspective—their view of what must be done should be based not on where they sit in the organization, but on where the organization stands on the battlefield; and

- a singularity of purpose—they have one objective and only one, and that is to determine the cause or causes of the organization's setback in candidate quality.

With that focus, they can identify the best path to victory: in this case, ever increasing numbers of ever more qualified candidates.

- **Third, war time leaders figure out how to win.** Analysis must lead to direction. War time leaders use their mental map to craft a strategy and a set of supporting tactics that will carry the day. How is this battle plan developed, in the midst of incredible pressure and with the sure knowledge that a misstep can trigger sudden and potentially devastating defeat? In part, of course, it is based on the training and skill of the leader. Successful generals are experts in their profession and practice their art continuously. Increasingly, however, military scholars acknowledge that successful battlefield decisions are also based on instinct or intuition.

Indeed, the reality is that, despite sensors and observations at the tip of the spear, the fog of battle is never completely swept away. Much remains unknown and unknowable in combat. Therefore, great battle plans are not simply the completion of detailed checklists based on guides or manuals. They are not simply the divination of right answers, using computer models or the scientific collection and reduction of data. That approach makes eminent good sense in the laboratory and, of course, in MBA schools. It is the basis of modern management theory. And it works just fine . . . in peace time.

In times of war, however, leadership is the art of making decisions without all of the answers. Instead of neat mathematical models, it is the leader's intuition or gut instinct that often provides the best guide. This seemingly untutored approach is actually just the opposite, for it involves both the shrewd assessment of a difficult situation based on one's experience and the application of the wisdom derived from that experience to formulate a concept of operations with a high probability of success. Intuition without those two elements is simply guesswork; and decision-making with intuition takes courage. In essence, then, the best insights about the direction to take are those inside the battle-wise leader at the tip of the spear. Indeed, official U. S. Marine Corps doctrine now recognizes intuition as the best approach to decision-making in the fog of battle.

- **Fourth, war time leaders make it happen.** The most successful combat commanders are able to convey their battle plan effectively to those who can implement it. They have both a clear notion of just what information must be transmitted in order to transform their strategy into action and the verbal and written communications skills necessary to do so. Major John M. Vermillion, in his article "The Pillars of Generalship," writes:

  > "At the operational level, the general must possess the power, derived from clarity of expression only, to knife through thick layers of command to be understood. Superior commanders at the operational level almost universally have been guided by a concern and talent for clear literary exposition."

  Does this statement mean that great generals are actually closet novelists, cranking out long treatises about what should be done, where and how on the battlefield? Absolutely not. The Army teaches tactical commanders to document an entire battle plan in just five paragraphs. They are:

- 1. Situation
     Enemy
     Friendly

- 2. Mission

- 3. Execution
     Concept of the operation
     Mission of elements, teams, and individuals
     Coordinating instructions

- 4. Administration and Logistics

- 5. Command and Signal (communications)

And in many cases, particularly in the heat of combat, the orders are even more encapsulated than that.

For example, General Heinz Gaedcke was a German Army commander on the Russian front in World War II. His unit fought in numerous engagements, and during every one of them, he carefully saved all of the documents he used to convey his orders to his subordinate commanders. Later, after the war, he went back over this archive of battlefield communications. At the conclusion of that review, he wrote:

> "To actually operate using formal written orders would have been far too slow. Going through the staff mill, correcting, rewriting, and reproducing in order to put out a written order would have meant we would have been too late with every attack we ever attempted. . . . It was a most peculiar feeling to see the orders, all very simple, that I had written in pencil so that the rain would not smear them— and each had the radio operator's stamp to confirm that they had been transmitted."

Long memoranda, fully staffed and reviewed operational plans, and the coordination and meetings they require are the luxuries of a unit in a peace time environment. In war, communications are an essential element of the plan of attack. They are part and parcel of how victory is achieved. They transfer the vision of the leader to those who will see that it is implemented in operations.

Human Resource leaders must, therefore, communicate just as clearly, succinctly and powerfully as the best war time generals. That is the only way they will be able to direct their units to the timely and decisive actions required for victory in the War for Organizational Security, the War for Trust and the War for the Best Talent. They must tell their subordinates precisely what they want done and ensure that they fully understand those directions so that they can be carried out effectively. Both steps are essential to success on the battlefield, and both are the responsibility of the leader.

The best war time leaders move forward to the tip of the spear in order to see the conflict in its starkest detail. Once there, they erect an inner fortress—a position of resolve and intense concentration—that can withstand the shocks of battle around them. This position becomes their vantage point, a psychological redoubt from which they can discern what must be done, fix their unit on that course of action and ensure that it never deviates. In times of peace, such leadership behavior might seem single-minded or even obsessive; in times of war, it is the focus required for victory.

WHAT MUST HR LEADERS & PROFESSIONALS DO?

 Be fanatical about collecting intelligence. What is happening in your organization in each of the theatres? What precisely is the status of the enterprise in the War for Organizational Security, the War for Trust and the War for the Best Talent? Equally as important, what is the disposition of forces (internal and external) that are or might be arrayed against HR in these conflicts?

 Analyze the data to determine what it will take to influence the point "where the crisis of action is going to happen" in each theatre. What are the factors that will leverage HR performance at those points? Which of those factors can HR control or best influence? What will it take to do so?

Devise a battle plan for each theatre. What specific actions should your unit take on what schedule to advance your department's cause in the War for Organizational Security, the War for Trust and the War for the Best Talent? Who in HR must do what to implement those plans? What resources and other support will they require to be successful?

Clearly communicate your plans to your subordinates and colleagues. What information must you provide for them to understand both your analysis of the situation and the course of action you have devised? What instructions are necessary for them to know precisely what they must do and how they must do it?

Act. Move to the tip of the spear and ensure that your battle plans are implemented correctly. Be willing, however, to adjust the plans as necessary to reflect changing conditions. Always deliver the support your subordinates require and steel their determination to succeed. And most importantly, never accept anything less than victory, from yourself and from those around you. Replace anyone who cannot or will not perform, as necessary, to achieve that end.

Selfless

Possessing the Soul of a Warrior

elflessness is a trait with two important facets. The first is a leader's willingness to sacrifice for those whom they lead. The second is their refusal to place their own welfare ahead of that of their subordinates. In an era of widely reported and even celebrated egocentrism, selflessness is the abnegation of "me first." In an era of "what's in it for me," this attribute is a commitment to the collective well being of those who are led. In an age of hyper self interest, selflessness acknowledges that organizations and their missions can advance the vital interests of us all and thereby repay our allegiance.

This characteristic clearly runs full counter to today's executive pay for performance culture. The quid-pro-quo paradigm works in peace because it provides a reasonable way to coax the best out of leaders. Bonuses, stock options and special retirement packages are individual inducements for individual contributions that can, in the absence of a threat, be summed to organizational measures of success. In theory at least, loyalty to oneself helps, rather than harms, the organization.

In a time of war, however, the calculus of commitment is

very different. Peace is about individual opportunity; wars are about collective threats. What does that mean for HR? The War for Relevancy is an attack on the value, purpose and future of the entire Human Resource profession. As such, it is a threat to each and every Human Resource professional, regardless of their personal circumstances at the moment. Fail in our mutual defense, and we won't lose our jobs, we will lose our careers.

The only way to win any war—and the War for Relevancy, in particular—is with personal sacrifice and tenacious effort on behalf of those with whom one serves. To put it another way, wars are won only by organizations working as one, not by one—even one who is very talented and charismatic—working within an organization. While individual perform-ance is clearly still important, the key to victory is the leader's ability to induce the members of an organization to subjugate their personal interests and even their well being to the mis-sion, itself, and to the benefits that will accrue to the organi-zation and its members with its accomplishment.

How does a leader draw such extraordinary behavior out of people? Generals do so by sharing a special bond with their subordinates, a bond called the soul of the warrior.

Warriors are among the few groups in the workforce whose everyday job requires extraordinary behavior. A core competency of their profession is to go above and beyond. They are not, however, asked or required to achieve that high standard all by themselves. Despite all of the mythology to the contrary, warriors are not solitary figures—some sort of Rambo or an army of one—striding across the battlefield. They are, instead, people who do their jobs in units. They are individuals who voluntarily agree to share two precious articles of faith: they accept a bond of shared purpose and they make a commitment to serve and support one another in accomplishing that goal.

The soul of the warrior, then, is:

- a kind of connectedness that one feels with others in a unit, a spiritual drawstring that is the antithesis of today's highly celebrated "golden handcuffs" approach to corporate allegiance; and

- the determination to work within that unit to achieve its objective(s), regardless of the personal consequences.

In essence, true warriors—the men and women in America's Armed Forces, for example—set aside their personal interests and even their own well being and devote themselves, instead, to one another and to their collective purpose.

Moreover, they do that, despite being paid significantly less and earning far fewer benefits than their private sector peers. It is a shameful situation, to be sure, but it is also reality. Warriors make personal sacrifices and herculean efforts on behalf of their unit without any expectation of financial gain. And that raises an important question: given our seemingly universal culture of self interest, how do warriors—with absolutely no opportunity for personal enrichment—come to this sense of devotion to one another and to their unit and its mission? Where does the extraordinary behavior of soldiers on the battlefield come from?

The answer, of course, is the caliber of the leadership that directs their work. Not the power of some hierarchical authority, not the influence derived from senior rank or title, not the logic of management strategy. No, the sacrifice and commitment of warriors is derived from the actions—the personified values—of the first among them. In effect, warriors are led to extraordinary behavior by emulating the behavior of their leaders.

The best war time leaders activate selfless performance among their subordinates by acting selflessly. They subjugate their own interests and well being to those of the unit. Ironically, accepting such a downsized personal claim on the organization actually enhances a leader's stature and clout in the organization. By diminishing their own opportunity, they increase their credibility and respect among those whom they lead. In the eyes of those around them, their self is not less, but more. Much more.

They are viewed as being in service to their profession and to the people of their organization. And that service— that commitment to act on behalf of those with whom they share a spiritual connection—builds a corresponding loyalty and determination within their subordinates. It fuels their willingness to go the extra distance required for victory in difficult circumstances. It energizes their commitment to serve the military unit or the business unit and its mission.

How is such subjugation of personal interest demon-strated by the leader? Normally, it occurs in two ways:

- **First, great war time leaders are willing to make the ultimate sacrifice.** Clearly, it takes selflessness as well as courage to place oneself at the tip of the spear, to be out in front of one's unit in the exercise of leadership. In that position, leaders symbolically (and, sometimes, actually) stand between their subordinates and the danger of action. They consciously accept the greatest exposure to threats and situate themselves so as to shield their followers as best they can. They do so, not because they are indifferent to their own welfare, but because they place the welfare of others above their own. In other words, selflessness is an active, not a passive state, regardless of whether it occurs on the battlefield or in the modern enterprise. It is the liv-ing out of the preeminent value a leader attaches to the organization and the people they lead.

  General Robert E. Lee showed such selflessness at the Civil War Battle of the Wilderness. On the second day of the campaign, the Confederate lines were dealt a devas-tating blow. If the lines buckled, Lee knew that the way would be open for Union troops to assault the vulnerable rear of his army. Fearing the worst, he ordered the supply trains to retreat and rode forward into the action. When he reached the battle lines, he spurred his horse past the trenches of General John B. Hood's Texans and into the smoky cacophony of the fight.

According to eye witness accounts, Hood's soldiers were transfixed by the image of "ole Marsh Robert" astride his horse, positioning himself at the tip of the spear and between them and the advancing Union army. His selfless disregard for his own personal safety steeled their determination in the face of extreme danger and gave them the will to fight on. They rallied, turned back the Union attack and saved the Confederate Army of Northern Virginia.

This subjugation of personal interest was also shown by more contemporary leaders in the face of an extraordinary constraint as well as battlefield danger. Although America's women have accompanied men into battle since the earliest days of the Republic, it wasn't until 1902 that Congress made them official members of the country's Armed Forces. Even today, they are not permitted to enter certain occupational fields in the military that could possibly take them into direct combat. As a consequence, while there have been a small number of women appointed to the rank of General Officer, not one has had the opportunity to command troops on the battlefield.

That situation, however, has not precluded women from demonstrating their willingness to make the ultimate sacrifice. During the war in Vietnam, thousands of women served in that country, mostly as nurses. And whatever the official government policy may have been, they were in the thick of combat each and every day. As one lieutenant colonel in the Women's Air Force (WAF) later wrote, "Dragon ships, helicopters and jets were firing from the skies; fire and smoke were all over the place. We even had a number of snipers in the immediate area.

One shot out the side of our bedrooms and must have continued down the halls."

In the face of such danger at the tip of the spear, these military nurses showed they too possessed the soul of the warrior. As one nurse recounted, "In the beginning, I could hardly move during a rocket attack. But you got used to it in a way—to your own fears—you had to. There was too much to do to dwell on it."

For example, during the Tet Offensive in 1968, North Vietnamese troops launched a ferocious surprise attack on a number of key American positions. The fighting produced a flood of casualties that quickly threatened to overwhelm the field hospitals near the front. To make room for them, a single Air Force nurse (who, to this day, wishes to remain anonymous) and her crew flew mission after mission over a three-day period and evacuated 1,500 wounded soldiers from bases throughout the country. Their routes of flight often took them over hostile territory where they were as much a target as the soldiers on the ground. Their willingness to put themselves in harm's way ensured that medical support would be available for their comrades on the battlefield.

Such selflessness under fire may seem foolhardy, especially to those who misperceive management as leadership. However, the allocation of an organization's resources and the supervision of its resource utilization—no matter how well executed—cannot and will not carry the day in war. Even the superior direction of people who dutifully come to work each day and do their jobs is not sufficient to produce victory on the battlefield. That end, whether it's sought among the rolling hills of northern Virginia, the rice paddies of Vietnam or in the modern office towers of an enterprise at war, can only be achieved with individual qualities that many say have all but disappeared in corporate America: unwavering unit loyalty, uncompromising devotion to duty and unstinting personal effort.

When a leader demonstrates the supreme measure of selflessness, they induce a mirror image of that behavior among those whom they lead. Subordinates see themselves in the actions of their leader, for they share the soul of the warrior. As a consequence, they accept their own subjugation into one unit, they act to serve the mission of the unit first, and they work with all of those apparently forgotten qualities of personal sacrifice because their leader—their fellow warrior—has led the way.

- **Second, great war time leaders model selflessness by holding themselves accountable for the actions of their subordinates.** As strange as it may sound, the soul of a warrior also entails the leader's unconditional surrender . . . not of the battle, but of any excuse or claim to mitigating circumstance in its outcome. Unlike politicians, great war time generals do not spin situations to find a more appealing version of events. Unlike lawyers, they do not craft arguments to develop plausible alternative versions of the truth. The best of these leaders, publicly and without caveat, accept full responsibility, both for their own actions and for the actions of those whom they lead. They affirm, by statement and deed, that it is they who set the standards for their unit's operations, it is they who make the decisions which guide those operations, it is they who oversee the conduct of the operations and, therefore, it is they who are accountable for the consequences, whatever they may be.

General Dwight D. Eisenhower provided a powerful example of such behavior. As the Supreme Allied Commander in Europe during World War II, it was Eisenhower who planned and launched the D-Day invasion on June 6, 1944. This amphibious assault on Nazi Germany's Fortress Europe was the largest and most complex military operation in the history of humankind. It involved hundreds of thousands of men and women in thousands of units with hundreds of different objectives and countless unknown variables in weather, terrain, human condition and chance. It was an endeavor sure to create the fog of battle on a monumental scale.

With so many unknowns and so much beyond his control, there were limits to what even a five-star general could do to ready his forces. Despite months of careful planning, thorough preparation and continuous practice of all phases of the assault, Eisenhower knew that, in the end, there was no guarantee that the mission would succeed. On the eve of the invasion, therefore, he penned a brief paragraph that both acknowledged an Allied defeat and took full, personal responsibility for it. Although he never had to send the message, his words are the epitome of selflessness among great generals at war. He wrote:

> "Our landings in the Cherbourg-Havre area have failed to gain a satisfactory foothold and I have withdrawn the troops. My decision to attack at this time and place was based upon the best information available. The troops, the Army and the Navy did all that bravery and devotion to duty could do. If any blame or fault attaches to the attempt it is mine alone."

Insulating themselves from the consequences of their unit's work and dodging responsibility when things go bad undercut a leader's credibility in the eyes of those whom they lead. They suggest a sense of self importance that weakens the bonds of unity and commitment to service required among units at war. They are the incontrovertible evidence that a leader is not willing to make the sacrifice he or she is asking of those whom they lead. Most damaging of all, they are the telltale signs of uncontrolled fear—

the ducking, disgraceful behavior of a coward. And, cowardly behavior on the part of a leader is the agent of cynicism and diminished loyalty among the led. It is the one sure way to mortally wound the soul of a warrior.

Eisenhower, in contrast, never flinched or ducked. Symbolically, he stood at the head of his army and, on the eve of the most important battle of his life, wrote a message that demonstrated the selflessness he was asking of his warriors. Just as important, he wrote it, not as some distant leader apart from the campaign, but as a member of the unit that would execute it. He pulled tight the spiritual drawstring and joined them on the beaches and cliffs of Normandy. He was one of them, whatever the outcome.

The message is also important, however, because Eisenhower wrote it, not for himself, but for the unit. His words were intended to protect those whom he led. He knew that a defeat in combat would inevitably bring out the home front critics, those who sit in judgment far from the danger of the battlefield. And, just as Lee rode out in front of his troops to protect and rally them at the Battle of the Wilderness, just as a single nurse and her team risked their own lives to save the lives of their fellow soldiers on the battlefields of Vietnam, Eisenhower symbolically strode out in front of his force and shielded its members from the slings and arrows of those who would fault their devotion and their effort. It was an act of selflessness that—had the message ever been issued— would have heartened the souls of his warriors so that they might rally to fight and win another day.

In its best expression, therefore, selflessness is the active combination of two other attributes—courage and focus. It is bravery without regard for the personal consequences of one's actions and a focus on preserving and protecting those whom one leads. It stands in marked contrast to the base behavior of corporate executives who have cheated on their taxes, negotiated extravagant retirement packages, walked away from their employers and employees with undeserved severance payouts and earned bonuses even when business is down and workers are being laid off. Indeed, selflessness is so rare in today's modern enterprise that it is often mistaken for folly or ineptitude. But it is neither of those.

Selflessness is the purest expression of true leadership, for leadership—especially leadership in the most trying of times—is nothing less than a leader's service to those whom they lead. It is the leader's acceptance of both a profound, personal responsibility for the welfare of their subordinates and an unconditional commitment to act on their behalf. Great war time leaders know that they must step forward to model the personal sacrifice and accountability they ask of others—they must show them the way—and defend their efforts to do no less—they must protect their passage along the way.

Leadership of that caliber can—indeed, will—re-ignite unit loyalty, devotion to duty and unstinting personal effort among the employees of the modern enterprise. Those values are not lost forever from corporate America. They have, instead, been misplaced by its leaders. And, selflessness is the key to their recovery. It is the standard of leadership that employees deserve and respect. It is behavior they can admire. Most important, it is the personal and professional exemplar they will follow, for instinctively they know that selflessness changes the scale in what they each and all do. It raises the bar of their own performance. The selfless leader draws them into a collective vision of what they can achieve and fuses them together so that they can reach up and grab it.

WHAT MUST HR LEADERS & PROFESSIONALS DO?

 Assess the soul of HR in your enterprise. How strong is the bond among your fellow HR professionals? What is their level of commitment to working as one? Do they feel a sense of responsibility to and for one another? Are they determined to work as a unit in waging the War for Organizational Security, the War for Trust and the War for the Best Talent? Is selflessness a core attribute of your HR department?

 Determine where you can act and what you can do to reinforce selfless behavior among your colleagues. Where can you step forward to be of service to your fellow professionals in each of the theatres of combat? What can you do to show them the way, to model the personal sacrifice and accountability required for victory? And, how can you protect them once they begin to follow your lead?

Put that knowledge to work. Subjugate your personal interests to those of the HR department. Adopt the War for Relevancy as your own struggle—it is. Serve your colleagues in that conflict by leading them with the unit loyalty, devotion to duty and unstinting personal effort required for your mutual success and by shielding them from those who would demean their efforts to emulate your example.

Humble

Always a Companion in the Foxhole

G iven their Hollywood image, it may be difficult to believe that humility is an essential character trait of war time generals. Indeed, the popular image of these warrior-leaders is probably that of the actor, George C. Scott, and his made-for-the-theatre rendition of General George Patton's speech to the U.S. Third Army, prior to its movement into combat in France during World War II. In the opening moments of the movie, he strides onto the stage, resplendent in his medal-bedecked uniform and carrying a riding crop that was commonly known as a "swagger stick" in the military of the 1940's. Then, standing in front of a huge American flag, he delivers a soliloquy that is as self-absorbed as it is stirring. It is a memorable performance and devoid of even a trace of humility.

Be that as it may, the most successful generals have, in fact, been remarkably modest, even as they have achieved historic feats on the battlefield. They have been both measured regarding their own capacities and role and effusive about those of their subordinates. They recognize, of course, the key role that they play as leaders, but they are just as clear-sighted (and some would say, honest) about the contribution of those who follow their lead. They understand that the outcome of the battle and, thus, their personal success are ultimately determined by those who do the work—by their subordinates and the skill and determination they display in combat—and they are very respectful of that reality. It's an attribute that undoubtedly makes them more agreeable personalities, but even more important, it also plays a key role in shaping what generals do and how they do it, in the face of conflict.

War time generals who are humble about their own capabilities and contributions touch both those whom they lead and, ironically, themselves in very important ways.

- **They foster a sense of teamwork among those whom they lead.** Every general and every CEO articulates the importance of teamwork and the necessary contributions that every member of a unit must make in order for the unit to achieve its mission. Indeed, a unit, by definition, depends upon the integrated (i.e., unified) actions of its members, whether it is a business unit in an enterprise or a combat unit in an army. Leaders deliver that message time and time again within organizations in order to build both:

  - a common sense of purpose, a collective vision of success and of the strategy and tactics that will best achieve it; and

  - camaraderie, esprit and an ethos of mutual support which serve to encourage and enable the members of the team to act on that vision.

Those two factors, more than any other, empower the whole of a unit to perform at its peak.

For many executives, then, teamwork is an important principle of effective management; it is the way they achieve integrated, coordinated operations. For their subordinates, however, teamwork is something else altogether; to them, it is a relationship. It is the emotional tie that comes from sharing adversity and danger, from being companions in the foxhole. It is a bond that enables them to believe that any mission can be accomplished because they are not alone. It is the durability and continuity of kinship that make the seemingly impossible task possible, the all-but-hopeless situation still hopeful. For those who are led, teamwork begins and ends with the deeply felt sense of inclusion, mutual respect and trust derived from membership in the group. Mission accomplishment is important, but it is secondary to that experience.

Most workers want that emotional tie. Some actually crave it. Teamwork as a relationship, however, is a fragile creation. While it can (indeed, must) be catalyzed by effective leaders, it can just as easily be undermined and even destroyed by the leader who abuses it. That abuse can be physical, of course—asking too much of even the most dedicated of teams—but more often than not, it is psychological—it is the team's detection of a leader's insincerity about the importance of the team and the value of its work.

Why is that sincerity so important to those who are led? Because, fundamentally, teamwork subordinates the role of any one person and all people—including the general or the CEO—to the role of the unit in achieving victory. It builds on the subjugation of self-interest that comes from the soul of the warrior, reinforcing it with a common mission and destiny. That is the only way that teamwork works. It is humility in action. It trumps rank and individual achievement with interdependence and shared purpose. So, a team is real—it is a genuine description of a unit's ethos or approach to work—only if its leaders are truly humble. And their sincerity in espousing teamwork is the best indication workers have of a

leader's humility—their absolute and exclusive allegiance
to the mission and destiny of the team.

The litmus test of that sincerity is the alignment
between what leaders say and do about the team, inside
and outside the enterprise. If team members—be they
soldiers in an army or the employees of a corporation—
perceive a disconnect between their leaders' public and
private words and deeds, they will mistrust their sincerity
and reject their call for teamwork. Indeed, from the perspective of those in the team, such disconnects betray
the very sense of inclusion, mutual respect and trust—
the feeling of oneness—that define the team experience.
And, without those elements, the team and all of its members are doomed. Their common mission cannot be
accomplished; their shared destiny turns hopeless.

To avoid getting caught in such an untenable situation, those who are led watch those who lead them all of
the time. This surveillance is actually a form of evaluation; its purpose is to compare what a leader says and
does within the organization and in public in order to see
how well they match up. The approaches that subordinates take to judging those words and those actions,
however, are very different.

- **Deeds—Do Leaders Walk the Talk?** In their evaluation
of a leader's deeds, subordinates are most concerned
with how their team is treated. They want what leaders
say publicly about the importance of teamwork to be
made real by what leaders do privately, inside the organization. In other words, they expect their leaders to walk
the talk. When they do, leaders actually catalyze—they
bring into being—the emotional tie of the team and
thereby acquire for their organizations the performance
benefits that teamwork provides.

When they don't—when enterprise leaders articulate
the value of employee contributions in the media and

then act differently in the corporation, for example—workers see that dichotomy as the leaders' insincerity in their statements about the team. When leaders describe workers as assets and their unit's competitive advantage and then lay them off by the thousands to achieve short-term profit goals (and the huzzahs of Wall Street), workers see that disconnect as a mockery of the relationship among team members. When leaders characterize cuts in employee compensation and pension plan contributions as a shared sacrifice and then pay themselves huge salaries and bonuses, they see such hypocrisy as the antithesis of humility.

That lack of humility, in turn, leads workers to a single, inescapable conclusion: Their leaders value themselves more than they value those whom they lead. Their leaders see themselves as essential and their subordinates as expendable. Their leaders are not companions in the fox-hole and thus have neither the right nor the moral standing to call on the special purpose and power of the team.

Humble leaders, in contrast, walk the talk. They not only articulate the importance of teamwork, they act to nurture and preserve it. Take the case of General Terry Allen, the commanding general of the 104th (Timberwolves) Infantry Division in World War II. The unit was barely a year old when he took command in September, 1943. Allen, on the other hand, had led the storied 1st U.S. Infantry Division into combat on D-Day. He had considerable experience whipping a unit into combat readiness, and had earned the nickname Terrible Terry in the process. It was not, however, a negative label; the term referred to the general's rare mixture of hard-nosed leadership and respect for those whom he led. As one soldier put it, "he was tough on discipline, but would go to bat for his men with anybody."

In Allen's view, the key to transforming the 104th from a green unit into a capable combat division was teamwork, and he never passed up an opportunity to make that point.

He talked to his soldiers about it constantly, on conditioning marches, on the rifle range and during training exercises in the field. Just as importantly, they believed him. Why? General Norman D. Cota, who had been Allen's Chief of Staff in the 1st Infantry Division, was once asked that question, and he answered it with a telling observation: "It's just because he's so damned honest."

Those whom Allen led accepted his words at face value—they judged that he was walking the talk—because there was an alignment between his words and his deeds. He acted on his belief in teamwork. Day in, day out, he took steps to make teamwork work. And, for his subordinates, small gestures were just as telling as grand initiatives. Maybe more.

For example, during the bitterly cold winter of 1944, the 104th was on the attack in the Aachen sector of southeastern Germany. The weather was miserable; a combination of snow, sleet and rain made every step forward a frustrating battle with mud and the danger of frostbite. To protect his soldiers, General Allen directed his supply department "to do everything up to and including grand larceny" to get them dry socks. And, he didn't stop there. He ordered every subordinate unit commander and every other officer in the division to ensure that their soldiers never went a day without dry socks. Allen drove his entire chain of command into a state of dry sock mania, and his troops loved him for it. They watched him act; it was a small gesture, but it made him believable. From their perspective in the unit, he walked the talk about teamwork. That credibility, in turn, steeled their sense of common purpose on the battlefield. The 104th became the tip of the spear for the U.S. 7th Corps and led its attack across the Rhine River and into the heart of Germany.

- **Statements—Do Leaders Talk the Talk?** Those in the ranks also expect perfect alignment between what leaders say internally and what they say externally about the role of teamwork. As with their evaluation of leaders' deeds, if they see a misalignment, they will reject the leader's call for teamwork and, no less important, view their leadership far more critically. In their view, leaders who fail to talk the talk are disingenuous and, quite possibly, intentionally deceitful in their espousal of teamwork. Those who exhort their employees to work as a team and then rush off to celebrate their own contribution to the victory deny the relationship between leader and led. Whether that self promotion is directed at the boss outside the unit or to the public at large, they have rejected the subordination of self required for true collective effort. Their humility is a public pretense, a sham. They are nothing less than traitors to the companionship of the foxhole.

General Creighton Abrams understood the importance of talking the talk and lived by that principle, even after he retired from active military service. As the Commanding General of the U.S. Army in Vietnam during the conflict in that country, he was often on the receiving end of conflicting guidance from policy makers and more senior military leaders in Washington, D.C.. Although that lack of clear and consistent direction undercut his ability to lead on the battlefield, he did his best to help his soldiers see themselves as a team with a common and important purpose and to craft a strategy that made sense to them. It was a thankless, perhaps, even futile endeavor, but he did it anyway because he believed that the members of his army—the team he served—deserved no less.

Years later, another general officer urged General Abrams to write his memoirs, to tell the true story about how the Vietnam War had been waged. According to this officer, General Abrams would not hear of it. As he recounts their exchange:

"His reply was vehement, 'Never.' And when I asked why, he gave me two reasons—because memoirs become larded with the 'vertical pronoun' and because he would never reveal certain aspects of his service in Vietnam."

Eschewing the vertical pronoun is the hallmark of a humble leader. Compare the behavior of General Abrams to that of some retired, memoir-writing Chief Executive Officers in today's self-congratulatory leadership environment. The purpose of their books is not to set the record straight or to recount history-in-the-making; it is, instead, to tell the rest of the world how smart and clever they have been. And when they do that, their subordinates— their so-called "teammates"—know these leaders don't talk the talk. It's fortunate that they retired when they did, because their legitimacy as leaders—especially leaders in a time of war—is defunct, the casualty of a self-inflicted wound—hubris.

Great combat generals, in very marked contrast, are just as fiercely proud of what they and their units accomplish, but they are also doggedly self-effacing. This humility is not a made-for-media persona or a public relations ploy; it is, instead, the manifestation of their strongly held belief in the team. They eschew self promotion because they view their words and deeds regarding the team as a pledge. It is their vow, their solemn acceptance of an emotional tie to the team. It is their unequivocal acknowledgement of a deep and permanent relationship with its members. It is their expression—their personification—of the importance of the team's work within the unit.

- **Humility also has an impact on a general's personal war-fighting ability.** Humble leaders recognize their own limitations and accept that they must counter them, if they are to perform effectively on the battlefield. In essence, humility both:

- enables leaders to evaluate themselves and their units honestly and objectively; and

- gives them the strength of character to take whatever steps are necessary to bridge any gaps that are revealed by that assessment.

The first step is a kind of personal performance appraisal in advance, while the second is a proactive version of traditionally post hoc performance improvement programs.

As generals prepare to go to war, they must determine exactly what they can do and what they cannot, unless they acquire additional resources. Wearing rose-tinted glasses during the preparation for battle is the surest path to swift and devastating defeat. Hence, the best generals aggressively search for inadequacies in both their own knowledge and skill set and in the capabilities of their unit. They do not, however, view these deficits as weaknesses or shortcomings, but as conditions of battle, as the circumstances with which they must work. To them, looking for imperfections is the process by which they come to understand what they must do to reinforce their team's prospects for victory.

Making such evaluations, of course, requires considerable self awareness and candor with oneself. Historically, the most successful generals have known their own intellectual and physical limits and made whatever allowances were required to stay within them. If they needed sleep, they got it. If they needed relief from the stress of command, they found it.

For example, General George C. Marshall was Chief of

Staff of the U.S. Army during World War II. Every decision
he made had a real and potentially fatal impact on the men
and women at the front lines. As a consequence, he
believed that a key part of his job was to keep himself fresh
and thinking clearly for each and every situation. To do that,
he normally left his office by 3:00 p.m. each day and almost
never made an important decision later than that. Despite
his position as the most senior leader in the entire United
States Army during a period of grave danger to the nation,
he was humble enough to accept that he must husband his
strength for a long and arduous campaign.

It is also important to practice such self-awareness
in peace in order to identify reinforcing techniques
that may be required later, in times of war. This preparation creates habits that enable a leader to perform at
peak levels, even during the demanding and difficult
conditions of combat. General Douglas MacArthur did
just that in 1935, when he took command of the U.S. military mission to the newly created Philippine Common-
wealth. He kept a standing appointment every day for
the 9:00 p.m. show at a Manila movie house. As one
military scholar put it, "He did not care what was playing; he fell asleep as quickly as he sat down. He found
movie-going a convenient way to unburden himself, to
undergo a daily psychic housecleaning." It was also
MacArthur's way of practicing, in peace, behaviors he
might have to use in war. He created patterns in his day
that gave him the mental and emotional space he
needed to address tough problems. It was a habit that
later served him well during the long days of fighting in
the Pacific theatre of World War II.

Successful war time generals are also humble enough
to know what they don't know. They work incessantly to
fill gaps in their professional knowledge and to expand
their understanding and mastery of their field. As evi-

denced by George C. Scott's portrayal, the popular notion of General George Patton is hardly that of a self-effacing man, yet on the eve of the D-Day invasion, he sent the following advice to his son:

> "To be a successful soldier you must know history. Read it objectively. . . . What you must know is how man reacts. Weapons change, but the men who use them change not at all."

Patton believed that generals became great war time leaders by learning from those who had preceded them on the battlefield. Sure as he was of his own capabilities as a combat commander, he was humble enough to know that he had much to learn from the great leaders of the past and even from his own contemporaries. Though he was to become one of the most senior leaders in the U.S. Army during World War II, he saw himself always as a student of leadership and his profession.

Finally, the humility of great generals enables them to appreciate the complexities of modern combat. Battles are no longer waged (if they ever were) by one brilliant tactician outsmarting another on the grand chess board of combat. Today's war time operations— whether they occur on the battlefield or in the marketplace—are often spread out over great distances and unfold at warp speed. They involve very large numbers of people using a wide array of increasingly sophisticated technologies, and depend upon long and vulnerable lines of supply and support. It's hard enough to keep track of all that is happening on one's own side of the battle line; in combat, however, your opponent also "gets a vote," and their actions inevitably complicate the situation even further.

No single person can possibly be aware of the almost

infinite range of variables involved in such a complex endeavor. No leader can individually accomplish the planning, preparation and execution of the millions of individual tasks required for a modern organization to act as a team. And, no general or war time leader, by him or herself, can deal effectively with the unpredictability of such complexity in the fog of battle.

That reality, of course, is why organizational staffs came into being. A carefully selected and fully integrated staff extends a leader's capabilities and provides them with two key benefits. It enables them to:

- devote all of their time and energy to doing those things they personally do best, and

- avoid the potentially negative consequences of their own limitations by drawing on appropriate strengths found in others.

This is not leadership by committee, but rather the optimization of a unit's performance by marshalling the reinforcing strengths of specialists under the direction of a single leader. Indeed, the best staff officers are renowned both for the brilliance they display in their area of specialization and for their absolute and unwavering allegiance to the leader they serve.

It is not surprising, therefore, that even the most successful war time generals have a very high regard for the contributions of their staff. General Gerhard von Blucher, for example, was an accomplished Prussian general who was well served by his chief of staff, Count Neithardt von Gneisenau. After a long and distinguished military career, von Blucher was invited to receive an honorary doctoral degree at Oxford University. As he accepted his award, he remarked,

"If I am to become a doctor, you must at least make Gneisenau an apothecary, for we two belong together always."

Similarly, the British commander Field Marshall Bernard Montgomery called his chief of staff a "pearl of very great price," while General George Patton's chief logistician, the officer responsible for keeping his army fed, clothed and supplied, was often described as "the best quartermaster since Moses."

There are occasions, however, when even the most capable unit and smoothly functioning staff are insufficient to ensure success on the battlefield. When such situations arise, humble leaders are able to recognize them and find a way to address them effectively. In many cases, they turn to coalitions to add combat power and other resources to their own capabilities. In effect, they go outside their sphere of control and negotiate a common objective and plan with external forces in order to create a task-defined entity with enough strength and durability to accomplish the mission.

Helpful as that new capability is, however, coalitions bring their own leadership challenges. They seldom achieve the cohesion of a single organization because the aims and understanding, the biases and needs of the various coalition members are never exactly the same. In essence, coalitions are always imperfect teams. Hence, securing effective integration and coordination among them is critical to their success, and accomplishing that task takes infinite patience, perseverance, the willingness to compromise, and most importantly, humility on the part of the coalition leader.

There is probably no better example of that trait in action than in the leadership of General Dwight D. Eisenhower during World War II. As the Supreme Allied

Commander in Europe, he was responsible for integrating an enormous coalition of British and American forces operating throughout Europe and North Africa. The British press derided his role as nothing more than "friendliness in welding an Allied team," a rather timid version of generalship exercised far from the dangers of the battlefield. Eisenhower's diary, on the other hand, reveals a proactive and engaged commander who kept the coalition working together through his personal and active direction.

He wrote:

"I had peremptorily to order the holding of forward air fields in the bitter days of January 1943. I had to order the integration of an American corps and its use on the battlelines. I had to order the attack on Pantelleria. . . . We had a happy family—and to all the C-in-C's [unit commanders-in-chiefs] must go the great share of the operational credit. But it worries me to be thought of as timid, when I've had to do things that were so risky as to be almost crazy.—Oh hum—."

That final and very private exclamation—Oh hum—is the true evidence of Eisenhower's humility. He was determined to do whatever it took to achieve victory for his command, regardless of how vexing coalition management became or how oppressive a view of his own role it created. What was most important to him was not his own personal stature or public accolades, but the teamwork of his fractious coalition on the battlefield and the progress it made toward victory.

Great war time leaders, then, are courageous enough to lead from the tip of the spear. Once there, they are unflinchingly focused on determining and executing a battle plan that will produce victory. They are selfless in the prosecution of the plan, modeling personal sacrifice and devotion to one's fellow warriors both during the battle and the public assessment that always follows it. And they are humble enough to believe fully and passionately in the importance of teams and teamwork. As a result, they celebrate and support the teams they lead, and they accept and address their own shortcomings and those of their units in their quest for victory.

WHAT MUST HR LEADERS & PROFESSIONALS DO?

 Evaluate the statements you are making both inside and outside the organization. Are you talking about the teamwork your employer will need to win its War for Organizational Security, War for Trust and War for the Best Talent? If so, what are you doing to make those words real inside the organization? Are your external statements backed up with internal deeds? And, is what you are saying internally consistent with your external statements?

 Resolve never to go to war without all of the resources required for overwhelming victory. To ensure that you have what you need, conduct an audit of your own capabilities and those of your unit. Do you have the appropriate skills at the necessary level of proficiency to execute your responsibilities in each of the theatres? Does your unit have all of the capabilities it needs to prevail? If not, what are the deficiencies and how can they be corrected? And, once these deficiencies are addressed, what must be done to practice and hone the upgraded individual and team capabilities so as to ensure their optimal performance in the battles ahead?

 Extend your power base, as necessary, to win deci- sively in each of the theatres. Do you need to assemble a coalition to acquire the combat power necessary for victory? If so, what capabilities or advantages must you add and which organizations or individuals can best provide them? What must you do to maximize the common interests of the coalition members and minimize their differences? How can you encourage the coalition to act as a team?

Bold

Imbued With the Spirit of the Bayonet

Leadership may be a noun, but the best war time generals transform it into an active verb. In marked contrast to those who exercise leadership as "leadersleep," they are full of energy and drive. They do not sleepwalk through their positions of responsibility, but instead, use them to act decisively. Their goal is not action for action's sake, however, or to check off the items on a to-do list. War time leaders direct their units to "where the crisis of action is going to happen" and then boldly lead them forward to seize the advantage and exploit it fully. In short, they take action to make a difference, to achieve real and important objectives. They are bold in order to determine the outcome of the battle and, as a consequence, to shape the fortunes of their organization.

Such action is clearly fraught with danger. Bold leaders always make decisions and launch campaigns with imperfect information and often do so in the face of daunting circumstances and very long odds. No less important, they push ahead knowing full well the possible consequences for their unit and for themselves. In other words, bold generals understand and respect the peril around them; yet, they act anyway.

They take this initiative because they realize that victory in war often turns on doing what the opposition cannot or is

unwilling to do. Where others see only personal or organizational risk, successful war time leaders see the opportunity
for and the advantage of daring action. To them, the most difficult situations are not dead ends, but disruptions to be
bridged; the most onerous of hardships are not impasses, but
obstacles that must be hurdled. For bold leaders, desperate
circumstances are occasions not for defense, but for aggressive offense . . . for the spirit of the bayonet. In short, the
best war time leaders attack when others are afraid to move.

One of the best examples of such bold action was
General Douglas MacArthur's amphibious landing at Inchon,
during the Korean War. In the summer of 1950, the
American Army was reeling southward on the Korean peninsula, battered by a surprise and ferocious North Korean
Army assault. Casualties were high, morale was crumbling,
and the specter of defeat was real. As the commanding general in the Far East, General MacArthur was responsible for
developing a response that would check the North Korean
advance and save the American Army. After studying the battlefield, he concluded that the only way to achieve those
objectives was to launch an amphibious assault—a D-Day of
the East—and sweep in behind the North Korean forces.
Such a strategy had the potential to surprise the enemy,
shock it off balance and, as a result, diminish the impact of
its numerical superiority on the battlefield. It was a bold
plan and, of course, extraordinarily dangerous.

Initially, MacArthur's staff identified three alternative sites
for the invasion: two on the west coast and one on the east
coast of Korea. Although all three options were conveyed to
the Pentagon, MacArthur, himself, quickly settled on his
choice: an attack at Inchon, a city on the western coast of
South Korea that was just 18 miles from its capital, Seoul.

The final selection of the site, however, was to be a joint
decision. In effect, MacArthur had to sell his choice to both
his superior officers in the Pentagon and to the leaders of the

other American forces that would form his coalition on the battlefield. These included the Air Force, which would be responsible for providing air support to the troops on the ground, and the Navy, which would use its Marines to clear and protect the beach and its sailors to land MacArthur's fighting units and their equipment. Although the military preferred to call it a "combined arms team," this coalition was, in reality, a classical ad hoc taskforce in which each member had its own parochial views of how best to achieve victory.

No sooner had MacArthur presented his case for the invasion site, than he ran into stiff opposition from both the Navy and the Marine Corps. They argued strongly for a different location, citing a number of serous risks at Inchon. Its harbor was small and its low tides posed a threat to the amphibious ships that would land the troops. Indeed, the invasion was planned for September, and there was only one day in that entire month when the high tide at Inchon would be deep enough to put water beneath the Navy's landing craft.

Despite these arguments, however, and the wariness they fostered among his superiors in the Pentagon, MacArthur never wavered in his view that the landing must be made at Inchon. His concept of the battle was undeniably risky, but it was also very opportunistic. After the troops had landed and moved inland, they would form an anvil against which the American forces already in Korea would launch a counterattack and hammer the North Korean Army. In effect, they would force the enemy to fight on two fronts simultaneously, thereby eliminating the advantage of its much larger force. They would also choke off the flow of supplies from its home bases in the North and thus weaken its ability to fight. In MacArthur's view, that was the one, best way to turn back the North Korean advance <u>and</u> save the U.S. Army in the south.

MacArthur's debate with the Navy and Marine Corps raged on throughout the summer, and, despite pressure from his superiors, he refused to concede. He remained focused on the strategy that he believed would lead to victory and refused to accept any other. Finally, his arguments prevailed, and he was given permission to proceed.

On September 15, 1950, the assault at Inchon was launched. Over 70,000 American soldiers stormed ashore. Although the Korean defenders were caught by surprise, they quickly recovered and put up a stiff resistance. The American advance slowed, but did not stop. It took three days of intense fighting to move just eight miles inland. Nevertheless, by the dawn of the fourth day, it was clear that MacArthur's plan had worked. The invasion force was able to sever the North Korean supply lines and move in behind the bulk of its forces. At that point, the American Army in the south launched its counterattack and began to hammer away at the isolated North Korean forces. Pummeled from two sides, they quickly lost their effectiveness, and the tide of the war turned in favor of the Americans.

MacArthur's bold strategy proved to be the key to victory, but it would not have worked, were it not for two factors:

- **A clarity of objective.** From the first moment of the North Korean attack into South Korea, General MacArthur had a single objective that he pursued without compromise or rest: he was determined to defend South Korea. This goal, however, could not be achieved by holding on or by hunkering down. Though often repeated, it nevertheless remains true that the best defense is an effective offense. MacArthur knew, therefore, that the only way he could defend South Korea was to attack—to respond boldly to the threat.

   That response, in turn, had to be directed at the leverage points in the campaign and configured so as to capture and apply their advantage. Bold leaders identify those supporting tasks that are critical to mission success and then design a plan that will position their unit to achieve them. They do so by taking the mission apart to determine what will most influence its outcome and then reassembling it with operations designed to acquire that influence. This process of deconstruction and reconstruction is the way a bold leader minimizes, to the fullest extent possible, the risks inherent in their actions. By focusing exclusively on those points that will turn the tide of battle, the leader concentrates all of their unit's combat power where it will most contribute to victory.

To defend South Korea, MacArthur realized he would have to accomplish two critical supporting tasks simultaneously. Achieving one or even achieving one after the other was insufficient for victory. He had to find a way to do both at the same time. He had to protect and preserve the American Army so that it could fight another day even as he repulsed the Korean forces from their occupation of militarily strategic positions in the South. And, only the assault at Inchon had the potential to do so.

In MacArthur's view, the other invasion plans that were developed by his staff could not accomplish the requisite supporting tasks. One called for a landing at Kusan, 100 miles south of Inchon. MacArthur believed that this attack could probably relieve the pressure on the battered American forces in the South, but would not dislodge the North Korean Army from its key positions. The other, a landing on the northeastern coast of the Korean peninsula, might force the North Koreas to shift some of their forces out of the South, but not enough to save the American Army from further and even more severe losses. Either course of action, therefore, might achieve some success, but not a full victory. The mission would be left unfinished and, worse, the combat power available to complete it would be severely depleted by the fighting.

As a consequence, MacArthur was unbending in his conviction that the only acceptable plan was the one that accomplished both supporting tasks at the same time. It alone met the minimum requirements for absolute victory, and absolute victory was the only acceptable outcome. Therefore, he pushed ahead with the preparations for an Inchon landing, even as he fought his rear echelon battle with the Navy and Marine Corps to get it approved. Finally, his clarity of purpose and determined championship of its rationale carried the day, and his bold strike was authorized.

- **Full and aggressive preparation.** Boldness is not rash action. Nor is it action taken without a careful assessment of the resources required for victory and the accumulation and deployment of those resources. In essence, boldness is decisive action based on exhaustive planning. It is fearless behavior backed by careful preparation. For the leader, therefore, the power of boldness depends upon priming the team, readying it to do its best.

  This preparatory effort is not confined to recognized requirements, however. Indeed, bold leadership—the ability to be decisive wherever the crisis of action occurs—depends upon preparation for both what is known at any point in time and what is not, for what is real and what can only be imagined. It may be accomplished to support a specific initiative, as was the case at Inchon, or it may be undertaken to plan for contingencies that may (or may not) occur in the future.

  For the Inchon landing, MacArthur realized that the timing of events had left him with a very small window for operations. The attack had to be launched in the early fall if it was to have any hope of achieving a successful conclusion before the arrival of winter in South Korea, with its significantly more difficult combat conditions. Therefore, even as he continued his debate with the Navy and Marine Corps, MacArthur ordered that planning for the Inchon assault move forward aggressively.

  His staff worked around the clock to develop the necessary operational plans; marshal and orient tens of thousands of soldiers; ready countless tanks, trucks and artillery pieces; and assemble the mounds of food, clothing, ammunition, tents and other supplies that the troops would need in the field. The fact that the invasion was launched successfully in the middle of September, meant that MacArthur and his staff had successfully accomplished a monumental feat of exacting preparation, all within the space of just eight weeks. It was their success in getting everyone and everything ready that laid the foundation for victory, on the beach at Inchon and beyond.

A very different kind of preparation played a significant role in one of America's most heroic stands in the European theatre of World War II. In December, 1944, Hitler launched a last gasp assault through the Ardennes Forest that caught the American Army off guard. In what has come to be known as the Battle of the Bulge, the German units pushed deep into the American lines, pinning units down in harsh winter conditions and cutting them off from their supply lines. Soldiers lacked proper clothing, ran low on food and ammunition and endured a ceaseless, ferocious attack by German tank and infantry units with larger weapons and more troops.

The 101st Airborne Division, one of this nation's most renowned combat units, was completely surrounded at the city of Bastogne and brutally hammered for days. As its lines shrank in the face of the relentless German advance, the American general on the scene, General Anthony McAuliffe, was told to surrender by the German force commander. His one word response to that ultimatum—"Nuts!"—was clear, brooked no misunderstanding, and rallied his troops to hang on.

Meanwhile, General George Patton's Third Army was advancing rapidly toward the heart of Germany. He had turned the German's own Blitzkrieg or "lightening attack" strategy against them and was rolling across France at an astonishing speed. His army of over 100,000 men and thousands of tanks and trucks had advanced 600 miles in just two weeks, battling the Germans every foot of the way, but always moving forward. Even as the army gained momentum and pushed through the German defenses, however, Patton's intelligence officer, Colonel Oscar Koch, began to worry about a German surprise attack through the Ardennes Forest. The generals in the head-quarters back in London scoffed at the notion, but Patton had great faith in his staff officer. He ordered Koch to develop all of the contingency plans necessary to blunt and ultimately repel such an attack. When it came, there-fore, the Third Army—alone of all of the Allied forces in the field—was ready to respond.

Patton then lead one of the most audacious attacks in the history of warfare. He stopped a huge army that was moving rapidly forward over hundreds of miles of terrain dead in its tracks. Next, he wheeled the entire mass of men and machines 90 degrees, and launched it toward the surrounded soldiers in the Bulge. Patton led the charge, not from his headquarters, but from his jeep—at the tip of the spear—at the head of the massive columns of roaring tanks and trucks.

As the miles rolled by, his driver, Sergeant Mims is reported to have said, "General, the army is wasting a lot of money on your staff officers. You and I can run the whole war from your jeep." Patton, however, knew better. Without the careful analysis of Colonel Koch and the expert planning of his staff officers, the Third Army would not have been able to respond to the threat. He had Mims pull to the side of the road, and as he watched his soldiers press forward, he remarked, "No other army in the world could do this. No other soldiers could do what these men are doing. By God, I'm proud of them." It was the highest compliment Patton could pay . . . to them and to the staff officers who had made it possible.

On December 26, 1944, lead elements of the Third Army made contact with the embattled soldiers of the 101st Airborne Division. They resupplied the hungry, worn out troops, and then pushed forward into the German lines. By the 28th of January, the battle was over. The German Army had been routed. The bulge in the Allied lines had been eliminated, by heroic fighting to be sure, but also by the less-than-glorious business of careful planning and preparation.

Great war time leaders act decisively. Audacious as their bold tactics may appear to be, however, those actions are not unreasoned or impetuous. They are, instead, based upon a carefully developed understanding of what supporting tasks are required for success, an unshakeable adherence to that vision and the in-depth planning and preparation necessary to achieve it on the battlefield. In reality, then, bold leaders are fearless in envisioning the path to victory—they will embark on a mission that others find too difficult or danger-ous—but they are meticulous in readying themselves and their units for its execution. They strike precisely at the point "where the crisis of action is going to happen" and with exactly the resources required to turn that crisis into victory.

WHAT MUST HR LEADERS & PROFESSIONALS DO?

1 Determine what constitutes absolute victory in your employer's War for Organizational Security, War for Trust and War for the Best Talent. What are the key supporting tasks that must be accomplished to achieve those objectives? What is the timing and sequence of the tasks (i.e., when must they be per-formed and in what order)? And, is the execution of

one or more of the tasks dependent upon the successful outcome of others?

Devise detailed plans of action and milestones for each of the theatres. What strategy and which tactics will best accomplish the tasks you identified in Step 1? What are the risks in each of these plans, and what must be done to minimize their potential danger? What obstacles are likely to be encountered in executing the plans, and how can they be overcome? What contingency plans should be devised to prepare now for potential threats in the future? And what metrics should be used to evaluate mission success, so that you can improve your unit's performance even as it moves forward.

Sell your plans to decision-makers by emphasizing the rationale with which they were devised. Aggressively champion the ability of each plan to accomplish specific supporting tasks that will, in turn, lead to full victory in each of the theatres. Be forthright in recognizing the risks inherent in your plans, but emphasize the preparations you have made to address them. And, once the plans are approved, ensure that all functional and business units in the enterprise are notified of the decision(s) and of their obligations to contribute to and support them, as appropriate.

Prepare for plan execution. What staffing levels and competencies must the HR department have in order to execute the strategy and tactics approved for each of the theatres (in Step 3)? In addition, what resources (e.g., technology, budget, information) will be required? How should the staff and resources be marshaled to ensure that they are available and ready for the start of each campaign? What follow-on and/or replenishment staff and resources are likely to be needed and how and when should they be acquired?

 Trust your plans and preparations. Exploit the opportunities they create. Do not allow progress to be slowed by difficulties or set-backs. Make adjustments, if necessary, but press forward relentlessly. Accept nothing less—from yourself and your colleagues—than the accomplishment of every supporting task and the achievement of absolute victory in each theatre.

Resilient

Unmoved by the Shocks of Combat

Wars are harsh, unforgiving events. Conditions are extreme, the hardships great. The shocks of combat percuss against the mind and senses, leaving one uncertain of what is happening or what should be done. But always, there is the sure knowledge that the stakes are very high, the price of a misstep potentially harmful or worse. Much is asked of those at the front lines, both leader and those who are led. They are thrust into the most difficult and demanding of circumstances, and still they are expected to advance and, ultimately, to prevail.

In such a cacophonous and perilous milieu, it is extraordinarily difficult to discern the best course of action. Leaders with differing responsibilities and agendas can (and, more often than not, do) arrive at very different visions of the situation on the battlefield and thus develop competing and even incompatible battle plans. Within any unit, therefore— be it an army or a corporation—the first step to victory is to settle on a single strategy that will then be fully supported by all of the components of the unit.

For the Human Resource department, that means it must:

■ devise the one strategy it will pursue in each of the wars it is fighting—the War for Organizational Security, the War for Trust and the War for the Best Talent; and

- ensure that its strategy—not that of any other functional area or of any business unit—is the one selected by the enterprise for execution in each of those conflicts.

And then, since there are always limitations to the resources that are available within the enterprise, HR must also:

- select the one set of initiatives—the specific tactics—that it will use to "operationalize" its strategy in each theater; and

- fight to ensure that HR receives from the enterprise both the priority and the support required for total victory.

In essence, the challenge for HR executives and for every war time leader is to win two conflicts:

- an internal battle <u>for</u> leadership, to determine whose vision of victory will guide the unit; and

- an external campaign <u>with</u> leadership, to implement the selected strategies and tactics and achieve full and lasting victory.

Winning the first conflict is a precondition for even participating in the second. Moreover, the battle for leadership does not end with strategy selection. Those who champion strategies that were not chosen will often counterattack as decisions are made regarding the allocation of resources. Hence, a successful unit is one that wins the battle for strategy and effectively defends the support it needs from the enterprise to execute the tactics that implement the strategy.

This "internal battle" to resolve competing plans and priorities among units and their leaders is no less real and central to victory than the fight with the enemy. It is not enough to be courageous and focused, selfless and humble and bold. All of those attributes can (and must) be present in a leader, and still, the battle will be lost, if the right plan of action with the right level of support is not selected. As MacArthur demonstrated at Inchon, fixing on the one best plan of operations is the critical start point in any campaign. Without success there, the war time leader loses the ability to affect the outcome of the conflict or even to play a meaningful role in its conduct. Indeed, the Human Resource profession will lose its War for Relevancy before the fight even begins if the enterprise fails to select its strategies and support its tactics in the War for Organizational Security, the War for Trust and the War for the Best Talent.

Even with the best of battle plans, however, the way to victory in combat can run through many twists and turns. There may be setbacks; sometimes, there is even a tactical defeat. But still the best war time leaders press on. As long as there is the faintest glimmer of hope, the smallest reason to believe that the ultimate victory can still be won, they never buckle. They are resilient in the face of adversity, unbowed by the shocks of combat. They may have to pause to give their unit time to regroup and re-energize for the fight; they may even have to order a temporary retreat. But, they never give up. They have an iron will to prevail. They are tenaciously devoted to victory . . . in both the battle for leadership and in the campaigns they direct with it.

Such resilience was amply demonstrated by General Joseph W. "Vinegar Joe" Stilwell in the Battle of China-Burma, during World War II. He arrived on the battlefield just after the Japanese Army had overrun Allied forces in the area. There were many casualties, and much equipment had been lost. His unit was in disarray. From the perspective of Stilwell's commander, the British General Harold Alexander, there was nothing for him to lead, so he ordered Stilwell to leave Burma immediately and set up his headquarters in Delhi.

Stilwell was offered a plane for transport, but refused both it and his orders back to Delhi. He explained to Alexander that to abandon his men at that moment would be devastating to their morale. The only way they would recapture their fighting spirit was to be shown that their setback was neither devastating to their cause nor a permanent state of affairs. They had to see the resilience they needed to be able to go on, so that's what Stillwell showed them. He assembled his force and marched out of Burma with them, covering 15 miles a day through dense jungle and heavy forests. It took weeks to reach Delhi, but by the time they arrived, every soldier knew that giving up was not an option. Once his troops were settled, Stilwell reported to General Alexander and was characteristically blunt in his assessment of what had happened:

> "I claim we got a hell of a beating. We got run out of Burma and it is humiliating as hell. I think we ought to find out what caused it, go back and retake it."

And, that's exactly what he set out to do. Stilwell earned his nickname by battling other generals in the theatre over strategy, supplies and priority. He was given command of a hodge-podge of units, including two depleted Chinese Army divisions. He developed a plan that would defeat the Japanese forces occupying northern Burma and cut a road from India to China, creating a potential threat to the Japanese islands from the west. It was an innovative, even brilliant strategy that opened what was later called a "back-door to Tokyo." In essence, Stilwell knew what it would take to win the external campaign, but first, he had to win the internal battle to lead it.

This preliminary conflict quickly grew fierce. There were at least three alternative strategies being pushed by other leaders in the Allied coalition. Each had their own vision and agenda, and all fought with Stilwell for priority and resources. His adversaries were General Claire Chennault of the U.S. Army Air Corps, who thought an aerial bombing campaign was the best way to expel the Japanese from the theatre, and the British General Orde Wingate, who argued for waging a guerrilla campaign against the Japanese Army in Burma. In addition, General Chiang Kai-shek, the Commander of the Nationalist Chinese Army, was pressing the U.S. Government to give Stilwell's equipment to him, under the Lend Lease program, so that he could attack the Japanese forces in China.

Even as these internal battles raged, however, Stilwell continued to reconstitute his army. He prepared as if he had been given the authority to proceed so that as soon as it came, he could. Midway through his preparations, however, a change of command put British Admiral Lord Mountbatten in charge of the theatre. Stilwell and the other commanders each pressed their cases, but Mountbatten refused to pick a single course of action. While pursuing several plans at once meant that no single plan could be fully resourced, all of the commanders were authorized to proceed, and in December, 1943, Stilwell launched his offensive back into Burma.

His first objective was the strategic airfield at Myitkyina. Thanks to a supporting action by Merrill's Marauders, an American unit lead by General Frank Merrill, he was able to take control of the Hakawing Valley. He then attacked and captured Myitkyina in May of 1944, but was unable to advance as the Japanese encircled and besieged his positions.

Stilwell asked for reinforcements, but was told that no troops were available. Those that could have supported him—General Wingate's Long Range Penetration Group and General Merrill's Marauders—had, instead, been committed to other strategies and, in the process, suffered heavy losses. Weeks passed, and still, no relief came. Concluding that his commander would not provide the support he needed,

Stillwell pressed his troops to fight on. They counterattacked, and after a fierce battle, finally broke the siege. Stilwell restarted his campaign to open a "Burma Road" to China and pushed further into Japanese occupied territory.

Meanwhile, Japanese forces had attacked and overrun U.S. airbases in eastern China, and communist forces under the command of Mao Tse-tung had gained control of most of northern and much of central China. To stabilize the situation, the U.S. military command wanted Stilwell put in charge of all Chinese forces. Chiang Kai-shek, however, would not acquiesce. Indeed, he blamed the Chinese Army's losses on the American decision to deny his Lend Lease request for equipment—equipment that had been given to Stilwell, instead. Faced with the dissolution of the Allied coalition in the region, President Roosevelt relieved Stilwell of his command and recalled him to Washington, D.C.. Despite this setback, however, he was still able to earn a promotion to four star rank and was reassigned to the Pacific theatre, where he served until the end of the war.

Stilwell grappled with a dispirited force, inadequate resources, waffling leadership, a lack of support in the field, and coalition politics, yet he never deviated from his pursuit of victory. He was a straight-talking leader who fought tenaciously for his objective, despite both internal and external shocks of combat. He quarreled with other generals, both Allied and American, and battled with the enemy, and always he pressed on. Even those with whom he crossed swords admired his resilience, and one—General Chiang Kai-shek—acknowledged his contribution to victory in the Far East by naming a part of the long route between Burma and China "the Stilwell Road."

Resilience, then, is an active state of mind and a state of action, in the face of difficult, even daunting circumstances. The shocks of combat do not paralyze resilient leaders, degrade their thinking or undermine their willingness to counter punch. They are tough skinned, tough on themselves and their subordinates, and very tough to derail. In storybook terms, these attributes are quintessentially American: confident, plain spoken, action-oriented and determined. On the battlefield, they describe "Vinegar Joe" Stilwell: uncompromising, acerbic, hard-headed and pushy. Whatever the point of view, however, resilience in a leader means the capacity to absorb whatever the enemy—internal as well as external—can deal and not be bowed.

No less important, that refusal to give up is not a one-time event. It is not limited to the first response to adversity, but instead, involves continuous effort until the winning strategy is found and implemented. That aspect of the attribute is what separates resilience from simply being obstinate. An obstinate leader pursues a single course of action whatever the consequences. In essence, their allegiance is to the strategy, rather than to the final outcome. Resilient warriors, on the other hand, are fixated on success, and they will strive incessantly to find the best way to achieve it. To put it another way, resilient leaders are serial searchers for victory.

Such was the experience of General John "Black Jack" Pershing, the leader of the American Expeditionary Force (AEF) in World War I. In September of 1918, the French Army was in full retreat as battle-hardened German forces arrived from the Western Front and rushed toward Paris. All that stood between the German Army and the French capital was the AEF's 400,000 American soldiers. It was an exhausted force, however, having endured heavy fighting in its victory in the St. Mihiel campaign just two weeks earlier. Nevertheless, Pershing agreed to return the unit to combat to defend Paris. His battle plan has come to be known as the Meuse-Argonne Offensive.

Pershing concluded that the best defense against the German assault was a counterattack in the area between the Meuse River and the Argonne Forest. It was not the most favorable of locations, but the German axis of advance left him little choice. The territory was a thick

tangle of forest and steep hills. And, the front, which
stretched for thirty miles, was fortified by defensive positions that the Germans had spent four years erecting.
Pershing did his best to prepare his troops, and on the 26th
of September, ten American divisions attacked, flinging
260,000 soldiers, 300 tanks and 500 aircraft into the battle
line. By the end of the first day, they had managed to
advance only three kilometers. The German strong point
of Montfaucon put up a determined defense and brought
the entire American force to a halt.

Pershing, however, refused to be deterred by this setback.
He reshuffled his forces and sent his most experienced
troops against the Montfaucon strong point. After fierce fighting, they were able to take the town, and the American attack
began again. In short order, the forward line of troops
entered the Argonne Forest, a seemingly impenetrable barrier
where the lack of roads all but eliminated the use of tanks.
The situation deteriorated even further as poor decision-making by a number of inexperienced unit commanders began to
produce severe casualties. In the west, the 77th Battalion—a
unit that came to be known as the "Lost Battalion"—was cut
off and isolated from the main body of the army. In the face of
these obstacles, the American advance, once again, slowed to
a crawl.

Looking for the right combination of fire power, tactics
and leadership, Pershing shuffled his commanders and repo-
sitioned his forces in the battle line. His changes were made
on the fly, but they worked. The reconstituted force began to
make headway again, even though German resistance
remained fierce. The campaign lasted six weeks and was still
underway when the Armistice and cease fire were signed at
11:00 a.m. on November 11, 1918. Although the Meuse-
Argonne Offensive saved Paris from German occupation, it
took a heavy toll on the AEF. A total of 26,277 Americans
were killed and 95,786 were wounded. The Lost Battalion,

surrounded and attacked ferociously for over six days, lost all but 252 of its 679 men before it was rescued.

The Meuse-Argonne Offensive, costly as it was, came to symbolize American resolve in the face of seemingly endless setbacks. As one historian wrote, "What the Allies were try-ing to achieve in over four years of brutal trench warfare, the Americans had done in only two months." How? By provid-ing their soldiers with leaders who never doubted the importance of total victory or their ability to achieve it. Leaders who were able to steel their units against every set-back and then find a way to battle through them. Leaders who would press every advantage to its fullest, even when it seemed as if doing so would exceed the limits of human courage and endurance.

And, why would these leaders do that? Because the best of generals know and accept two verities of warfare:

- the shocks of combat will always present the severest of tests—no battle is easy, especially those that are most important; and

- their own leadership must always be unflinching in the face of those challenges—they must never give up and must always press forward, if victory is to be achieved.

Why is such resilient leadership so important to the Human Resource profession? Because we, too, are at war. We face both internal and external opponents who do not believe HR is relevant in today's organizations and economy. We are under attack both in a fierce civil war for adequate budgets, staffing levels, resources, and priority within the enterprise and in an ever more aggressive barrage of commentary by crit-ics and prospective replacements outside the enterprise. And inevitably, in these battles, we too will experience tough chal-lenges, demoralizing setbacks and even tactical defeats as we struggle to protect and preserve our profession and role. That is the nature of combat, and it is the nature of our situation, as well. Hence, we cannot—we must not—give up.

The best war time leaders help those whom they lead to achieve that resilience. They devise battle plans that will work, and they lead their units steadfastly in the execution of those plans. Whenever adversity is encountered along the way—whenever the shocks of combat occur—they recover as quickly as possible, rapidly revise their plans to accommodate the conditions on the battlefield, and return to the fight. They are serial searchers for victory, and their unflagging effort—the steel of their character—reinforces the will of those whom they lead.

WHAT MUST HR LEADERS & PROFESSIONALS DO?

 Develop a clear understanding of the challenges you will face in leading your organization in its War for Organizational Security, War for Trust and War for the Best Talent. Which entities and/or individuals inside the enterprise will compete with or oppose your leadership? Why will they do so? What will be the likely nature of their opposition?

 Determine how best to counter the opposition. What are your strengths and how can you apply them to your advantage? What are your vulnerabilities, and how can you eliminate or, at least, minimize them? What are the vulnerabilities of your opponents and how can you take advantage of them?

 Be relentless in promoting your strategy and leadership role. Identify both the formal decision-makers and informal influencers to whom you should make your case. Use every form of communication and forum you can to present your position, and present it multiple times to each person. In describing your rationale, emphasize the strengths of your strategy and exploit the weaknesses of your opponents.

Implement your strategy in each of the theatres. Model the resilience you will need from your peers and subordinates to prevail in the War for Organizational Security, the War for Trust and the War for the Best Talent. Lead by doing whatever it takes—legally and ethically—to win. Then, keep doing it. If you run into difficulties, search for an alternative approach and make the appropriate adjustment. You may need to pause—to reorient, reorganize and/or re-energize yourself and/or the HR department—but never quit the battle until absolute victory has been achieved.

Inspirational

Seasoned With a Feel for the Troops

Wars, fortunately, are normally rare events. When they do occur, however, they create extraordinary demands on those involved. Their tests are out-sized; their consequences enormous. Though we would avoid them, we cannot retreat from their reality or their potentially cataclysmic impact on our present and future. Plato said, "Only the dead have seen the end of war." For the rest of us, they are sometimes inescapable challenges of enormous dimension, hazard and influence.

Wars cannot be won, therefore, with business-as-usual kinds of deeds. They require performance at a level far above the norm. Inspirational leaders help individuals and units ascend to that level. They enable them to reach for the very best of their talents in the face of awesome challenges. They empower them to make right decisions when doing so is the most difficult path to take. The best war time leaders inspire those whom they lead to perform tasks and achieve ends that are beyond ordinary human effort, for such acts alone have the power to achieve the high standard of victory.

How do leaders become inspirational? Emerson once said, "Our chief want in life is somebody who will make us do what we can." A U.S. Army recruiting theme from the early 1980's captured the same idea: Be the Best You Can Be. This desire to perform at our peak is an innate human drive, and inspirational leaders activate and energize it.

But what gives them the ability to do that? Where do inspirational leaders acquire the capacity to draw the best out of people? What is it that transforms a leader into a figure who emboldens others to perform extraordinary feats?

There are many misperceptions about the source of this all-too-rare ability. For example, inspiration is often thought to be the product of the position of authority a leader holds or of their seniority on the organizational chart. It is not. Nor is it derived from effusive press releases or public acclaim or even from stirring speeches. A leader's 15 minutes of fame or 30 minutes of verbal exhortation can produce 15 or 30 minutes of determined effort by their subordinates. They cannot fuel an individual's, much less a group's, determined reach for the high bar of sustained excellence. To put it another way, rank and words may motivate, but only deeds inspire.

Yet, even deeds may not be enough. Action for action's sake is nothing more than inspiration by roulette wheel. It happens by chance, not as the intended outcome of the leader. Inspirational leadership, on the other hand, is achieved by actions that purposefully show others how to raise the bar of their own performance. It comes from deeds that reflect the character of the leader. In essence, the ability to inspire others is based on both what the leader does and who they are.

Inspiration—the ability to draw out of people the potential each holds within them to perform above the norm—is only achieved when a leader earns the respect of his or her subordinates. The operative word in that statement, of course, is "earns," and as with so much else in leadership, it is an active verb. War time leaders inspire their units to extraordinary levels of performance by performing at those levels themselves. They have acted, and their deeds demonstrate—

they, themselves, model—the kind of behavior required for victory. They have shown courage at the tip of the spear. They have peered through the fog of battle and focused on the course to victory; they have drawn on the soul of the warrior to step forward selflessly in the face of danger. Yet, always, they have been humble in preparing and supporting their companions in the foxhole. They have drawn on the spirit of the bayonet to take decisive action in desperate situations, and they have been resilient when confronting the shocks of combat. These deeds are the currency of inspirational leadership. They are the way respect is earned.

Inspirational leaders give others a guide to follow and, in so doing, they ask as much or more of themselves as they ask of those whom they lead. There is no false bravado, no brave talk and then meek action, no double standard, no special treatment by virtue of position or rank. War time leaders inspire their followers to extraordinary levels of performance because they drive themselves to such levels first. They inspire by being the best they can be. They share the danger, the adversity, the fear, and they act anyway.

This sharing of experience creates a special sense of closeness—a complementarity—between leaders and followers.

- From the leader's perspective, this recognition of interdependence is a personal salute to those whom they lead and an acknowledgement of their key role in victory. In effect, it is a direct and public affirmation of a leader's faith in the character of their subordinates and their capacity for extraordinary feats. It is their way of saying, "I am no better than you, and I will show you what we can do."

- From the perspective of those who are led, the sharing of experience is the leader's diminution of self and a celebration of their mutual effort. It alone provides credible proof that the leader sees him or herself, not as some remote figure of authority safely away from the action,

but rather, as the first among a tight-knit band of warriors. It is their way of saying, "We see what you are asking us to do, and we will be as good as you."

In essence, the sharing of experience infuses the war time
leader with a feel for the troops and accords them the
stature and the right to ask for their best.

General George Washington demonstrated such inspirational leadership in the days immediately following the end
of the Revolutionary War. The victory had been achieved,
British troops had departed, and the 13 colonies had
become 13 independent states. Their union was not perfect,
however; they were still not yet a nation. There was no
Federal Government. The Continental Congress was strug-
gling to assert itself, but its authority was untested. It was an
unstable, even precarious environment that threatened to
deny the final achievement of a United States of America.

Fearing anarchy, a group of nationalists came to see the
Continental Army as the only cohesive, national institution
that could respond. By secret message, they urged its leaders
to launch a military coup and seize control of the fledging
nation. Washington emphatically refused. Although he was a
soldier and Commander-in-Chief of the Army, he believed
fervently in the democratic principles articulated in the
Declaration of Independence. Some among his officers,
however, thought the proposal had merit and called a private meeting to discuss it. Washington was invited to attend,
but declined.

On the day of the meeting, the men gathered in a hall not
far from their camp. Emotions ran high, and most of the rhet-
oric was strongly in favor of the Army's taking control of the
situation. There would be no fruits of victory, the nationalists
argued, if civic order was not maintained, and only the army
had the power and unity required to do so. Suddenly and
without announcement, Washington entered the meeting
hall. In the shocked silence that followed, he asked if he

might address the assembly. These men had risked their lives and those of their families when they marched off to war with him seven years before. Many had been under his command ever since, in the cold winter at Valley Forge, through the defeats at Brooklyn and Trenton, and finally in victory at Yorktown. He was one of them, and they quickly acceded to his request.

Washington began by reminding them of the long struggle they had shared and of the freedom they had achieved together. He went on, imploring them not to undercut that accomplishment by inserting the Army into the affairs of state. He acknowledged the difficulty of the situation, but argued that military action, however well intentioned, would destroy the very principles for which they had fought and so many had died. Then, he pulled from his pocket a letter that had been sent to him by the Continental Congress. As he prepared to read it, he looked around at his comrades-in-arms and said, "Gentlemen, you will permit me to put on my spectacles, for I have not only grown gray but almost blind in the service of my country."

That simple statement was, at one at the same time, both a reference to their shared experience and Washington's personal salute to his men. In showing his own vulnerability, he quietly asked for their strength, in defending the union they had won together. It was a remarkable demonstration of his feel for the troops, and according to witnesses, turned the meeting in an entirely new direction. Washington defused the incipient revolt and inspired his soldiers to preserve the liberty for which they had fought so hard and finally won. The meeting adjourned, the Continental Army disbanded, and the American principle of civil control over the nation's military was established. It is a principle that has guided the American Armed Forces ever since.

Is such a high standard of behavior really necessary in the Human Resource profession today? Are the issues and risks and challenges we face of a magnitude to warrant such extraordinary deeds? Does our mission in the enterprise have the solemn importance to justify the inspirational leadership necessary to be the best we can be?

People come into our profession absolutely convinced that the answer to every one of those questions is yes. They believe that people—not the power of technology, not the brilliance of strategic plans, not the clarity of financial analysis—are the engine of an organization's success. People operate, devise and apply those tools, and people, therefore, give them whatever power they may have.

As soon as HR professionals begin to work in an enterprise, however, the weakness of human capital in the marketplace of business priorities becomes apparent. Not in all organizations, of course, but in too many, people are an asset that is undervalued to the point of being disposable. Unlike facilities, financial capital and even intellectual property, human capital can be thrown away. And that reality—expressed in a constant barrage of inadequate budgets, staff cuts, ignored or discarded programs, slurs about the "touchy-feely" nature of our work and omission from key decisions and plans—chips away at the confidence of HR professionals. After awhile, they too begin to ask those questions, and based on their own work experience, wonder about the answers.

Moreover, the very existence of the questions bears witness to the genuine threat the HR profession faces in the War for Relevancy. This conflict is being waged, at least in part, as a psychological campaign within the enterprise. At its most basic, it is a battle for breathing space, a fight for survival—a conflict to secure a share of scarce resources, priority and management attention—among the functional centers of the modern corporation. In effect, the HR profession is under attack by those who would profit by its minimization or, better yet, its elimination. And their tactics of choice are confusion and doubt. They seek to undermine our own sense of worth and worthiness, our own belief in the centrality and high purpose of our calling.

The one sure way to fend off this assault is with inspirational leadership. Indeed, Human Resource professionals cannot be managed to victory in the War for Organizational Security, the War for Trust and the War for the Best Talent. The demands are too great, the risks too high, the consequences of failure too ominous for the standard operating procedures of peace time leaders. These are real and pressing battles, and we will only prevail with leadership that nurtures and unleashes our full potential. Human Resource professionals need and deserve inspirational Human Resource leaders who will model the attributes required to win. For, it is only by being the best we can be that all of us—leaders and led—will turn aside the nay-sayers and internal critics who are waging war against us.

Inspirational leadership, however, cannot be episodic or applied because events warrant and then forgotten as soon as they don't. It is not a strategy that a leader can use to achieve victory in a conflict and then ignore when that conflict is ended. It is, instead, the permanent, perpetual personification of the complementarity between the leader and led. It is the leader's living of that interdependence—their day-in, day-out expression of it—that accords them a feel for the troops and earns their respect. Indeed, the inspiration that enables great deeds to be performed is fleeting, and its basis—the respect of the led for the leader—must be re-earned every day.

The sad example of General Sir Charles V. F. Townshend illustrates this point. In late 1915, World War I was barely a year old. General Townshend commanded an Anglo-Indian force of over 13,000 troops that was battling the Turkish Army in what was then called Mesopotamia and is now the country of Iraq. Anxious to protect the oil fields in the region and to deflect public attention from the British Army's humiliating defeat at Gallipoli, the British military headquarters in London ordered General Townshend to effect a "regime change" in Baghdad. The general was highly regarded by his troops and, under his inspirational leader-ship, quickly gained battlefield success. They overran a num-ber of key tactical objectives, culminating in the defeat of a larger, better armed and heavily fortified Turkish force at the town of Ctesiphon, just 25 miles south of Baghdad.

The price of victory, however, was dear; 40% of the British troops were killed or wounded in battle. As a result, Townshend had no choice but to retreat back down the Tigris River. Unable to get boats or medical supplies, his soldiers endured a long, dusty, painful march that finally ended at the town of Kut, a river junction that Townshend had captured a month earlier. His troops could go no further, so they fortified the town and were quickly surrounded by a Turkish army led by German officers. The ensuing siege went on for over four months. At the end, British soldiers were eating cats and dogs, and the vegetarian Indians were down to seven ounces of grain a day. Over 1,700 of Townsend's men died. And yet, as one writer described it, Townshend "knew the value of morale, and until the end kept the respect of his men."

The end, however, was not the capitulation of the British force. The thousands of British and Indian soldiers who sur-vived the siege were then marched off to terrible treatment by the Turkish army. As one historian described it, "The men were herded like animals across the desert, flogged, kicked, raped, tortured, and murdered." The poet Geoffrey Elton, himself a survivor of Kut, later wrote of that terrible march into the desert, with "none of them fit to march five miles . . . full of dysentery, beri-beri, scurvy, malaria and enteritis; they had no doctors, no medical stores and no transport. . . ."

It was then, at the moment when his troops most needed inspiration, that General Townshend lost his way. Although he too became a prisoner of the Turks, he spent his captivity in a villa in Constantinople. In contrast to the wretched treat-ment endured by his troops, he lived in comfort. While they suffered, he was celebrated and even knighted by the British government.

During the war, Townshend was made out to be an inspirational hero; afterwards, as the contrast between his own treatment and that of his troops became known, his standing collapsed. He could no longer claim to have a feel for his troops. He had ignored the special closeness that drew them together and, as a consequence, forfeited the privilege of being a leader who had earned their allegiance and respect. General Townshend had ceased to be a model they wanted to emulate. Had those troops been re-committed to battle, he could not have led them, for they would not have followed.

To be truly inspirational, then, war time leaders must perform two critical deeds. They must show their respect for their followers by feeling as they do, sharing in their combat experience; and they must earn the respect of their followers by always being at their personal best, by offering an example worthy of their collective emulation. The led must see the leader as a person who is both one of them and an exemplar of individual acts that meet the highest of standards. In essence, the inspirational leader shows them what they are capable of achieving. He or she shows them the power and the promise of being courageous, focused, selfless, humble, bold and resilient. Then, he or she raises them up to that extraordinary level of achievement.

WHAT MUST HR LEADERS & PROFESSIONALS DO?

Review the other six attributes of effective war time leaders—men and women who are courageous, focused, selfless, humble, bold, and resilient. What actions can you take to express those characteristics, to personify them in your employer's War for Organizational Security, War for Trust and War for the Best Talent? Which of those actions are likely to have the greatest impact on the outcome of each campaign? And, which will offer the best models of what others in the Human Resource department can and must do to achieve victory?

 Perform the deeds that make a difference. Be the best you can be so that others can and will emulate your performance. Share their trials and pressures, their setbacks and advances. And, then, give them your personal example of what they can achieve with effort that reaches up to the highest standards and levels of achievement—in the War for Relevancy and in each of its three theatres.

Give yourself a regular "personal performance appraisal" to ensure that you are always modeling the attributes of an effective war time leader. Are you still being the best you can be? Have any of the conflicts in your organization so changed that you should alter the actions you perform to lead the way to victory? While the steps you take may (indeed, in all likelihood, will) change over time, the attributes—the personal characteristics you demonstrate—must not. They are the hallmarks of great leadership in difficult times. Make them your own.

Shock & Awe

From the HR Department

Its title notwithstanding, this book is not a paean to war. It is not meant to celebrate human conflict or to revel in the corporate civil war now facing the HR profession. It is not intended to preach jingoism in a business book or to set the HR department on the path of conquest in the modern enterprise. This book does not issue its call to arms lightly.

The truth is that no soldier ever wants to go to war. Unlike video game warriors, those who do the real fighting know the risk of combat. They are fully cognizant of the threat it poses to their present and future well being. And, still they go. They march off and do their duty because they believe they must—they are fighting for their country or for a transcendent set of principles—not because they see any glory in it. They do not look forward to the fight, and they hope and pray for its speedy conclusion.

Soldiers also know, however, that the greatest danger in war comes from waiting too long, from hoping against reason that the threats around us will go away of their own accord. Indeed, when we allow those who push us aside for their own interests to go unchecked, when we persist in inaction because we think those who belittle us will suddenly embrace us as partners, when we let the fear of potential consequences overcome our sure knowledge that many of today's corporate HR decisions and policies are wrong, then we accept defeat without contest. We volunteer for victimhood. We give ourselves no chance at victory because we never enter the battle, or more precisely, because we never summon the will to win.

That is the topic of this book. While it describes war and war fighting, it is about leadership. It is about the will to win in difficult times. It is about the Human Resource profession taking its rightful place in the modern enterprise. For, the only way we will achieve that end—the only way we will protect and preserve our present and future in the modern enterprise—is to fight back. In essence, we must push back the encroachments into our operations, turn back the claims to our competence and capacity, and win back our mission.

We must do that—we must exercise the will to win—because our profession has been and remains under attack. This description of our situation is not metaphorical; it is fact. Time and time again, we've been assaulted by the budget axe, the staff guillotine, the friendly fire of leaders who talk about the importance of workers and then desert them, and the barrage of commentary, inside and outside the enterprise, that denigrates our work and our principles. We have been confined to second class status in the enterprise, denied a role in its decision-making and strategy-setting and ignored when we raised critical issues or concerns.

For years, we have struggled to reverse this course through negotiation. We've tried reasoning with other leaders in the enterprise—to make "the business case"—and we've tried to act more like them—to be "strategic business partners." We've done all of that and more—and we've done it in good faith—but, it has been to no avail. We have never gained the acceptance, the respect or the trust of those who lead our enterprises. We remain the invisible person of the corporate leadership team, and worse, we now face expulsion, altogether, from the organization.

That threat represents the gravest danger to the HR profession in its history. It forces us to confront a stark and forbidding choice. Either we fight back or we surrender. Either we stake our claim to a meaningful role in the enterprise or we accept annexation by another function or by consulting and outsourcing companies. Either we take up arms or we give up. Either we find the will to win or we lose.

If we choose the latter course, we will act as our peers expect. We will go humbly into the night, accepting a future dictated to us by the traditional power centers in the enterprise. If, on the other hand, we fight back—if we say that we will stand by the principles we stand for—then we will take control of our own destiny. For the first time, we will set the course for our profession and its future. We will be in control of our fate.

But, how can we in HR do that? How can we—without the budget or the staff or the priority of our adversaries—hope to achieve this victory?

The answer is as profound as it is simple. We can win by changing our view of ourselves and our mission. We will win by being a different kind of HR.

First, we must stop asking permission to be proactive and engaged. We must no longer wait for others to come to our point of view before we act. We must no longer waste time in futile efforts to convince others of the importance of what we do or to change their minds through reason and compromise. That kind of behavior is the essence of diplomacy, and the time for diplomacy is over. Fifty years of evidence is enough. It didn't work. We are at war.

Second, we must stop defending ourselves and start taking offensive action to achieve the ends we seek. We must stop being process managers and rule keepers, and start being leaders who project real power at the leverage points in enterprise operations. We must stop guarding our turf and start encroaching on turf that has heretofore been the uncontested domain of our peers in the enterprise. In short, we must attack. And, we must fight to win.

We must accept no other outcome but victory. And that requires yet another change in HR, in us. Winning at war requires a special kind of leadership; it requires leaders of character, and that is what we must become. Now, don't misunderstand. HR professionals have always been highly principled people of character. Most of us have not, however, been leaders of our enterprises. And, as a consequence, we have not had the opportunity to develop and/or express the attributes of leaders, particularly those who know how to prevail in difficult times. So, that must be the first step in our mission. We must acquire the attributes of great war time leaders—of generals. And then, we must use those attributes to lead our departments and our profession to victory.

However, as this book's tales of generalship demonstrate, leaders of character do not win great battles by fighting for themselves. They prevail by fighting for others—for their country, for their unit and for their fellow soldiers. And, the same is true for leaders of the Human Resource profession. We must fight back by fighting for our enterprises. In their War for Organizational Security, their War for Trust and their War for the Best Talent. Those are their struggles—and they are real and monumental challenges—yet, we must make them our own. For, when we accept that role, we will be the change we want to see in the world. When we fight for leadership in these wars and then win them, we will impose shock and awe on our adversaries inside and outside the enterprise. And, when we do that, we will win our War for Relevancy.

ABOUT THE AUTHOR
AND WEDDLE's

Peter Weddle is the Editor & Publisher of WEDDLE's a niche publisher that specializes in the Human Resource field. In addition to his books on HR leadership and management, he also edits annual Guides and Directories to the 40,000+ job boards and career portals now operating on the Internet. Known for their accuracy and helpfulness, these publications led the American Staffing Association to call him "the Zagat of the online employment industry."

The editorial foundation of WEDDLE's can be described in a simple phrase: People Matter Most. All of its publications as well as Weddle's seminars and presentations and his consulting are built on the premise that strategic advantage—in business or any other collective endeavor—can only be achieved and sustained by effective human capital formation. This "workforce wealth," in turn, is derived from highly principled leadership and management practices vastly different from the conventional wisdom of public market makers.

For more information about WEDDLE's, please visit its Web-site at www.weddles.com or call its offices in Stamford, CT at 203.964.1888.